Problem Solving 101

The Art of Business Strategy and Execution

John P DiBiasi

TABLE OF CONTENTS

Introduction

Problems arise in various shapes and sizes. Some can be solved easily, while others may not be immediately identifiable. Some require special skillsets, and others demand intuitive insights. This book aims to equip the reader with the skills necessary to solve real-world business problems by applying the power of observation, logic, and critical thinking. The topics covered offer techniques and skills applicable across a spectrum of real-world problems.

Most of us are not fond of books or articles that could have been just as useful in half the number of pages. Following the example of Niccolò Machiavelli's "The Prince," this book's approach is to condense a wealth of advice, insights, and wisdom into as few pages as possible without compromising value for brevity.

In writing this book, I have drawn upon more than 40 years of practical experience across a wide number of industries and businesses in both leadership roles and as a consultant to many well-known companies. While there is no substitute for experience, creativity, and hard work, some problem-solving skills can be learned.

Problem-Solving at a Large Scale Involves Human Behavior

Not every problem comes down to science, engineering, mathematics, logic, and technical skills. Often, we find that we need to rely on others to solve with us or for us. This means that an entire set of skills for dealing with individuals and organizational behavior comes into play. So, in addition to building general problem-solving skills, knowing a bit about human behavior is necessary.

The Manhattan Project, the secretive endeavor to develop the atomic bomb, presented as much a challenge in cultivating teamwork among brilliant and often eccentric personalities. The science and engineering explored the limits of theoretical physics. But the ability to meld different skills and personalities into cooperative teams led to a solution. Recognizing the human element may help you solve problems more quickly.

After all, if every problem were purely mathematical, we would have a greater need for mathematicians!

By combining practical experience, problem-solving skills, and an understanding of human behavior, this book aims to provide readers with a comprehensive toolkit to tackle complex challenges. Whether you are a seasoned professional or just beginning your problem-solving journey, the insights and wisdom shared in this book will guide you through the art and science of problem-solving.

So, let's embark on this journey together, as we uncover the power of observation, logic, and critical thinking to solve real-world problems in modern strategy and organizations. Prepare to enhance your problem-solving skills and unlock your potential to overcome obstacles and find innovative solutions.

1.   The Elegance of Simplicity

It's easy to complicate problems and solutions more than necessary. While some problems are inherently complex, like designing a spacecraft for a lunar mission, others have straightforward solutions waiting to be identified.

In our pursuit of solutions, we often fall into the trap of complexity, mistakenly believing that intricate solutions are inherently superior. However, overdesigning and overcomplicating solutions can hinder progress and lead to unnecessary costs and delays.

Consider a software developer designing a customer records database. It's tempting to include numerous future-oriented fields or collect more information than necessary. Such tendencies lead to overdesign and may create additional challenges later.

Complexity can also emerge when solving problems. Choosing the most intricate solution may make us feel accomplished or intelligent, but it often comes at a high cost. Extended project timelines, increased resource allocation, and mounting expenses can all be the unintended consequences of such an approach.

We must heed the adage, "If all you have is a hammer, every problem looks like a nail." This reminds us to pursue the simplest solution that effectively addresses the problem. Often, the simplest solution is the most effective one.

Embracing simplicity has numerous advantages. Simple solutions typically have fewer moving parts, reducing the chances of failure. They require less effort and resources, resulting in cost savings. Moreover, they often have fewer steps, increasing the likelihood of success.

However, it's critical to recognize that not all problems in the corporate world can be resolved with simple solutions. Many challenges are complex and multifaceted, demanding a more nuanced approach. For instance, launching a small business involves a myriad of interconnected challenges, including funding, personnel, marketing, and sales.

In the face of such complexity, it becomes crucial to navigate the chaos and transform it into order. Developing a well-defined plan is the first step towards this goal. Breaking down larger problems into smaller, manageable components allows for sequential or parallel problem-solving.

Whether tackling a problem solo or leveraging a team's collective intelligence, establishing clear boundaries and defining responsibilities is crucial. Eliminating duplication and streamlining the process fosters simplicity in both design and management.

The more precisely a problem is defined, the more quickly individuals can understand its intricacies and contribute to a solution. By clearly communicating the problem, whether it's a strategic plan, a project, or a series of unrelated tasks, you enable others to align their efforts effectively.

Ultimately, problem-solving should be approached with clarity and logic. When the path forward is evident and rational, individuals are more likely to follow and contribute their expertise to finding elegant and practical solutions.

In the pursuit of solving complex problems, always remember the value of simplicity. Embracing simplicity as a guiding principle unlocks potential for streamlined processes, efficient resource utilization, and successful outcomes. Allow simplicity to be your beacon on the path to effective problem-solving.

Example: The Over-Engineered Widget

Imagine a company, Widgets Inc., that creates widgets. They began with a simple product that was loved for its ease of use and reliability. Over time, the company's engineers, driven by the desire to innovate, started adding features.

Some of these features were driven by customer feedback, but many were added in anticipation of future needs or because they seemed like impressive technological advancements.

Fast forward a few years, and Widgets Inc. released their latest model: the WidgetX. It was a marvel of engineering with capabilities ranging from weather prediction to language translation. The problem, however, was that most customers simply wanted a widget to do what it had always done efficiently and without fuss.

The WidgetX, with its overabundance of features, was intimidating to use, had a steep learning curve, and was prone to malfunctions due to its complexity. Sales began to decline, and customer satisfaction dropped. The additional features, rather than adding value, were detracting from the core functionality that had made the widget popular in the first place.

Realizing their mistake, Widgets Inc. decided to return to their roots. They released WidgetS — a stripped-down version of the widget that focused on core functionalities with a user-friendly design. It was an immediate hit, restoring the company's reputation and profitability. WidgetS proved that simplicity could meet customer needs effectively, leading to a better product and a stronger market presence.

This example serves to show that complexity for its own sake often does not serve the customer or the company and that a focus on simplicity can lead to better outcomes. It provides a concrete scenario to which readers can relate and which reinforces the message of the importance of simplicity in problem-solving and product design.

2.   Choosing Which Problem to Solve First

When faced with multiple problems, it's natural to feel overwhelmed and unsure where to begin. The stack of challenges before us can seem insurmountable, but it's important to remember that even the most complex problems can be broken down into smaller, more manageable components.

Defining success becomes crucial. Before diving into problem-solving, take a moment to envision what success would look like for each problem. By setting clear goals and objectives, you provide yourself with a target to strive for and a means to measure progress. Defining success also helps align efforts and ensures that everyone involved understands the desired outcome.

Equally important is defining failure. Understand that not all endeavors will lead to success, and that's acceptable. Recognizing the indicators of failure allows you to assess when your efforts are not yielding the desired results. Embrace failure as a learning opportunity and be willing to pivot or abandon an approach to save time, resources, and energy. **Know when to throw in the towel and move on**.

As you examine the array of problems before you, adopt a strategic approach. Understand the broader context, long-term goals, and overall vision. This strategic thinking will guide your decision-making and ensure that your actions are aligned with your larger objectives. At the same time, embrace tactical thinking – the ability to focus on immediate steps and actions that will move you closer to your goals.

Resource allocation plays a vital role in your efforts to solve problems. Assess the availability and limitations of your resources, including finances, time, expertise, and human capital. Prioritize the most critical problems and allocate your resources effectively, ensuring alignment with your priorities.

To illustrate the importance of effective problem-solving within resource constraints, consider the world of house flipping. Flippers face a myriad of problems, such as repairs, renovations, marketing, and financial considerations. Success in this competitive field relies on the ability to balance resources, set priorities, and make strategic decisions to maximize profitability.

Beware of the "squeaky wheel" issue — the tendency to focus solely on the most vocal or urgent problems. While it's tempting to address these issues immediately, neglecting other important matters can have long-term consequences. Prioritize problems based on their urgency, impact, and alignment with your strategic objectives, ensuring that all critical matters receive the attention they deserve.

Prioritize your lists of problems, tasks, or issues ensuring that the details don't overshadow the overarching strategy. Regularly reassess your priorities and review progress, adjusting your focus to ensure continuous attention to problems and steady progress towards their resolution.

Complex Problems Lend Themselves to Being Solved as a Series of Smaller Problems

Breaking down a daunting task into manageable components allows for a more systematic and strategic approach to finding solutions. By deconstructing the main issue into smaller, interconnected challenges, individuals can focus on addressing each one with clarity and precision. This method not only enhances problem-solving efficiency but also provides a clearer path towards achieving the overall objective.

This enables a strategic allocation of resources, time, and expertise, ensuring that each subproblem is thoroughly analyzed and resolved before moving to the next.

In this way, the intricate web of complexities gradually unravels, paving the way for a comprehensive and successful resolution to the initial complex problem. By taking a step-by-step approach and carefully addressing each component, you can maintain a sense of progress and build momentum towards the ultimate solution.

Example: "Just like Jigsaw Puzzles"

Imagine a software company facing the daunting task of developing a complex new application. At first glance, the project appears overwhelmingly intricate, with numerous interdependent features and systems that need to integrate seamlessly.

To tackle this, the project manager breaks down the application into smaller, manageable modules. Each module represents a specific functionality or a component of the application, such as user interface design, database management, or security protocols.

By segmenting the project into these smaller parts, the team can focus on solving individual challenges one at a time. This approach not only simplifies the development process but also allows for more thorough testing and refinement of each module.

As each part is completed and tested, it can be integrated into the larger framework, gradually building up to the complete application.

This method of breaking down a complex problem into smaller pieces is akin to solving a jigsaw puzzle. Instead of trying to piece together the entire picture at once, a more effective strategy is to start with small sections.

For example, one might begin by assembling the border, then grouping pieces by color or pattern, gradually filling in the gaps. Each small victory of fitting pieces together builds momentum and clarity, eventually revealing the whole picture.

In the context of our software development scenario, as each module is developed and integrated, the team gains a better understanding of how the different parts interact and complement each other.

This incremental progress not only makes the problem more manageable but also provides frequent milestones and successes, keeping the team motivated and focused.

3.   Solving the Right Problem

Identifying a problem is the crucial first step in the problem-solving process. It involves recognizing the existence of an issue or challenge that needs to be addressed.

It may seem obvious, but it's amazing how many times people ignore or overlook the problem right in front of them. By developing a keen sense of observation and a proactive mindset, you can become better at identifying problems early on and taking prompt action to resolve them.

In some cases, a solution itself can be problematic. It happens when the implemented solution does not fully address the underlying issue or creates new complications. It's important to critically evaluate proposed solutions and assess their potential consequences to ensure they align with the desired outcome. Sometimes, reassessing the solution and refining it can lead to better problem-solving outcomes.

The question often arises: Is a void better than a bad solution? When faced with an unsatisfactory solution, it may be tempting to discard it entirely and start from scratch. However, the absence of any solution can also have its drawbacks. It's essential to weigh the costs, benefits, and potential risks associated with both options. Striving for a balance between the two is key to finding the most effective approach.

When searching for a solution, it is crucial to consider the possibility that the problem may not be where you initially thought. It's easy to get fixated on a particular aspect or area, potentially missing the root cause or an alternative perspective. By maintaining an open mind and being willing to explore different angles, you increase the chances of uncovering hidden problems and finding innovative solutions.

If the Problem Isn't Where You're Looking, It's Somewhere Else

Have you ever found yourself searching a drawer over and over, hoping to stumble upon a missing item? Problems often persist because we keep approaching them the same way without considering alternative methods. Embracing creativity, experimentation, and a fresh perspective can help break free from this cycle and discover new solutions that were previously overlooked.

Not all problems require immediate attention and intervention. It's important to recognize that some issues may resolve themselves over time.

While it's essential to monitor and assess the situation, expending unnecessary effort and resources on transient problems can be counterproductive. Focus your energy on the problems that truly require your attention and intervention.

Prioritization is a fundamental aspect of problem-solving. It involves identifying and addressing problems based on their impact, urgency, and scale.

By tackling problems with the most immediate impact or the ones that affect a larger scale, you can maximize the positive outcomes of your problem-solving efforts. Establishing clear goals and objectives helps guide the prioritization process, ensuring that your actions align with your desired outcomes.

The significance of clearly identifying the right problem to solve and prioritizing your steps or goals to address it cannot be overstated.

By honing your problem recognition skills, avoiding the pitfalls of overlooking or misjudging problems, and assessing solutions critically, you can set the stage for successful problem-solving endeavors.

Remember to keep an open mind, think creatively, and focus on the problems that matter most in order to achieve your goals.

Example: Solving the Right Problem in Tech Support

Imagine you're at the helm of a tech support team for a software company. Customers have been reporting that your flagship product crashes intermittently, which is becoming a growing concern.

Initially, the support team's response has been to advise customers to reinstall the software—a straightforward, quick fix. Despite this advice, the problem continues to occur, leading to mounting customer frustration and a potential hit to your company's reputation.

In line with the strategies outlined in this chapter, you recognize that simply addressing the symptom—software crashes—with a temporary solution is not truly solving the underlying problem. To uncover the root cause, you shift the team's approach to a more detailed investigation.

You encourage your team to meticulously observe and log the circumstances surrounding each crash, seeking patterns that might reveal the deeper issue at play. While this investigation is underway, you provide customers with temporary workarounds, which helps to alleviate the immediate inconvenience without leaving them in a lurch.

As your team analyzes the collected data, a revelation comes to light: the crashes are not due solely to an issue within your software but are triggered by a conflict with a recent update from another widely used program.

This conflict is what's causing your product to fail. With this new understanding, your team steps out of the conventional troubleshooting box and develops a patch that cleverly circumvents the issue, effectively stopping the crashes.

While the team's focus is on this significant problem, they also identify a few minor bugs. However, you recognize that these are less critical and seem to be resolving as your team enhances the software. Deciding not to divert resources to these minor issues allows you to focus on more pressing matters.

Understanding both the impact of the software crashes on the user experience and the urgency of the situation, you prioritize the rollout of the patch. You also make sure to communicate openly with your customers about the steps being taken to resolve the issue.

By concentrating on the real problem—how your software interacts with a changing digital environment—you not only remedy the current issue but also lay down a framework for anticipating and resolving future software conflicts.

This proactive stance not only resolves the immediate technical crisis but also strengthens customer confidence in your product's reliability and your company's commitment to support.

4.　Focus on the Solution, Not the Problem

Let's delve into the importance of adopting a solution-oriented mindset in problem-solving. It's crucial to discern whether the identified problem is the root cause or merely a symptom of a deeper issue.

With complex problems, it is important to strike a balance between understanding the cause and taking action to avoid excessive analysis, which can be wasteful. We need to steer clear of the dangers of over-introspection, which includes finding someone to blame, and instead shift towards an action-oriented approach.

Additionally, we want to focus on the positive elements, minimizing blame, and fostering a collaborative environment. By embracing these principles, individuals can enhance their problem-solving skills and achieve more effective outcomes.

Is What You Are Focusing Upon, Really the Problem?

As you sit there, staring at the issue that has been plaguing you for weeks, you can't help but question if you're concentrating on the right problem. It feels like a never-ending cycle of firefighting, with no real resolution in sight.

That's when you decide to step back and reassess the situation. You begin asking probing questions: Is this problem just a symptom of something deeper? Are there underlying dynamics at play that have not been considered?

By digging deeper and challenging your assumptions, you come to understand that the focus of your attention might not be the real issue. It's merely a manifestation of something larger and more intricate. This insight shifts your perspective.

You redirect your efforts toward comprehending the true problem, which leads to devising a more precise and effective solution. This experience underscores the significance of critically examining the situation and not settling for addressing superficial problems.

Identifying the Cause Can Sometimes Be a Waste of Energy, Money, & Time

In your pursuit to find the root cause of a problem, you might find yourself descending into an abyss of endless analysis. Each new discovery leads to further questions, investigations, and, consequently, more resources squandered. It becomes apparent that you are caught in a cycle of over-analysis, which prevents decisive action.

At this point, you choose to pivot your focus. Understanding the cause is important, but not at the cost of delaying the solution. You decide to pursue a pragmatic approach.

Rather than continuously dissecting the cause, you begin to explore potential solutions and test them iteratively. This approach is freeing, and you feel a surge of momentum and progress.

By finding equilibrium between understanding the cause and initiating action, you manage to make concrete steps toward resolving the problem while keeping future prevention in mind.

Avoiding Over-Introspection

Buried in data, reports, and analysis, you might feel swamped by the volume of information gathered. This is the trap of over-introspection: analyzing every detail to an exhaustive extent and spiraling into a loop without reaching a conclusion.

Realizing that this introspection is stalling progress, you choose to break away. While analysis is valuable, it must be balanced with action. You consciously shift toward solution generation and proactive implementation steps.

Embracing an action-oriented mindset allows you to utilize your insights effectively, free from the paralysis of excessive introspection. This approach clears the way for a more dynamic and successful problem-solving journey.

Everyone Wants Credit, Few Accept Blame: Focus on the Positive

During problem-solving discussions, it often becomes clear that people are keen to claim credit for successes but reluctant to assume responsibility for failures. This attitude can create defensiveness and hinder the collaborative process. In recognizing this, you take steps to redirect the team's focus.

You start to shift the conversation from blame to recognizing positive contributions. You encourage your team to consider their strengths, available resources, and viable options. By promoting a positive focus, you create a conducive environment for collaboration and innovative thinking.

Example: Redirecting a Project Review Session

In the aftermath of a product launch that didn't meet expectations, the product development team gathers to review the outcomes. The mood is initially defensive; team members are quick to highlight how their contributions were successful, while subtly suggesting that the failures lay outside their domain.

The conversation is teetering on the brink of a blame game, which threatens to undermine the team's camaraderie and future collaboration.

Recognizing the potential for lasting damage, you intervene to steer the discussion in a more productive direction. You acknowledge the disappointment openly but remind everyone of the innovative features the team managed to implement successfully. You highlight specific instances where team members went above and beyond, demonstrating commitment to the project.

With this redirection, you then encourage the team to reflect on the strengths they each brought to the project. You ask them to consider how these strengths can be leveraged for future initiatives and what resources proved most valuable during the development process. As each member contributes their insights, the conversation naturally evolves from one of fault-finding to one of resourcefulness and resilience.

By the end of the meeting, the team has compiled a list of positive takeaways and learnings, not just a litany of missteps.

The focus on what can be built upon rather than what went wrong helps to restore a sense of unity and purpose.

The team leaves the meeting with a renewed commitment to apply their collective strengths to upcoming challenges, turning a moment of potential discord into a stepping stone for growth and innovation.

5.   Defining Constraints and Establishing Trade-offs

In problem-solving, constraints are the boundaries that define the scope of our solutions. Understanding the limitations and conditions we face allows us to approach problems with clarity and focus. Defining constraints involves pinpointing the specific factors that restrict our options and influence the problem-solving process.

These constraints can be categorized into natural constraints, which arise from the inherent characteristics of the problem, and artificial constraints, which are deliberately imposed to stimulate creativity.

Recognizing and defining these constraints deepens our understanding of the problem landscape and enables us to explore innovative approaches within established boundaries.

Artificial Constraints

Artificial constraints are intentional limitations we impose on ourselves to spark creative problem-solving. By deliberately restricting resources, time, or other parameters, we challenge conventional thinking and promote innovative solutions.

These constraints can lead us to think outside the box and consider unorthodox approaches. For instance, setting a strict time limit or reducing available resources can push us to find efficient and creative solutions.

However, some artificial constraints may unnecessarily hinder the identification of solutions by imposing arbitrary or capricious factors. While they can foster creativity, there's a risk of limiting the solution space with constraints that lack a clear rationale.

It's important to strike a balance when implementing artificial constraints, ensuring they aid in stimulating creativity without unduly constricting the problem-solving process. By critically evaluating and adjusting artificial constraints, we can exploit their benefits while avoiding the pitfalls of arbitrary limitations, allowing for a broader exploration of potential solutions.

Time, Money, People, and External Factors

Resource constraints are pivotal in problem-solving. Time constraints necessitate efficient management to ensure solutions are realized within deadlines.

Financial constraints require judicious allocation of funds to maximize value while curtailing costs. People constraints take into account the skills, availability, and collaboration potential of the individuals involved in the problem-solving process.

External factors such as legal regulations, market conditions, and environmental considerations significantly influence the available solutions or options to address a problem.

These factors introduce additional complexities that must be considered. Legal regulations can dictate permissible approaches or limit actions.

Market conditions, like supply and demand or competitive forces, influence the feasibility of solutions. Environmental considerations, including sustainability or ecological impact, define the acceptable range of solutions.

Understanding and navigating these external factors is crucial for ensuring compliance, adaptability, and the development of sustainable solutions that adhere to broader societal, economic, and environmental goals.

When is it Permissible to Deploy a Temporary Solution?

Deploying a temporary solution is permissible when it addresses immediate needs or mitigates urgent issues, serving as a stopgap until a more permanent resolution is found.

For example, a truck fire in June 2023 led to the collapse of a bridge on the heavily trafficked I-95 corridor in Philadelphia. Normal construction for a bridge takes months.

To provide an immediate, albeit short-term, resolution, the area beneath the bridge was reinforced to allow for a temporary roadway and the highway was swiftly reopened. While a long-term solution is in progress, the temporary measure fulfilled the immediate goal of restoring traffic flow.

Temporary solutions are often necessary when constraints of time, resources, or complexity preclude an immediate comprehensive resolution.

Nonetheless, the impact, risks, and feasibility of temporary measures must be carefully considered. They should be assessed against long-term objectives, with plans to ensure a seamless transition to a permanent solution. The benefits of temporary solutions can impact overall costs while achieving immediate objectives.

Competing Priorities

Competing priorities, which refer to conflicting objectives that must be managed simultaneously, are a common challenge in problem-solving. Balancing cost efficiency with high-quality outcomes is one such example.

Successfully managing these priorities requires clear goal definition, prioritization based on impact and urgency, and the pursuit of win-win solutions where feasible.

In the I-95 bridge example, there were three primary concerns: reopening the highway promptly, ensuring the new structure met current codes, and managing overall costs effectively.

The temporary reopening was achieved quickly, albeit with the understanding that it might extend the timeline and budget for the permanent structure.

It's essential to identify which priorities are paramount compared to lesser goals. High priorities are those that demand most of our attention and resources as they contribute directly to core objectives or require urgent action.

Lesser goals, while still important, may not have the same immediacy or impact on the final outcome. By discerning and defining high priorities, we ensure that significant objectives receive adequate attention and resources, while still addressing secondary goals in a balanced way.

Placing Boundaries Around a Problem

Setting boundaries around a problem is an essential step in problem-solving. Defining the scope and limits prevents scope creep and ensures a focused approach.

Boundaries based on core objectives, resources, time, and feasibility considerations help maintain clarity, facilitate effective analysis, and guide the problem-solving process toward meaningful outcomes.

When we face a challenge, it's often tempting to dive right in and tackle every aspect of the issue head-on. However, without first setting boundaries around a problem, our efforts can quickly become unfocused, inefficient, and ineffective.

Boundaries serve as guardrails to keep our problem-solving efforts on track, ensuring that we address the core issues without being sidetracked by peripheral concerns.

Defining the boundaries of a problem requires us to establish clear parameters that outline what is within the scope of our current efforts and what lies beyond them.

This delineation is crucial for several reasons. First, it provides a clear understanding of the problem's extent, which is vital for formulating a targeted strategy. It allows team members and stakeholders to have a shared understanding of what the problem is—and, just as importantly, what it is not.

In practice, setting boundaries may involve stipulating which resources are available and which are off-limits, determining the time frame for addressing the issue, and specifying which potential solutions are viable based on ethical, legal, or practical considerations.

For instance, in product development, boundaries might include the technology currently available, the budget allocated for the project, and the regulatory standards that the product must meet.

These constraints focus the creative process, prevent mission creep, and ensure that the team doesn't waste time pursuing avenues that are unfeasible or outside the project's intended scope.

Moreover, by placing boundaries around a problem, we also set the stage for measuring success. When we have a clearly defined scope, we can establish specific, measurable objectives.

These objectives then inform the criteria we will use to assess whether our solutions are effective. Without such boundaries, it can become nearly impossible to gauge progress because the goalposts are constantly moving.

However, it's important to remember that while boundaries are essential, they should not be so rigid as to stifle creativity or prevent the reevaluation of the problem if new information comes to light.

The boundaries we set should be seen as dynamic and adaptable to change. As new data becomes available or as the situation evolves, revisiting and, if necessary, redefining the boundaries can be just as important as establishing them in the first place.

6.   Time Changes the Nature of Problems

Time plays a crucial role in transforming the nature of problems we encounter. As the clock ticks, what once seemed like insurmountable obstacles often morph into trivial concerns, while seemingly minor issues can grow into significant challenges.

This temporal shift in the gravity of problems is not just a matter of perception but a reflection of the dynamic interplay between changing circumstances, technological advancements, and societal evolution.

For instance, consider the realm of technology. A decade ago, the challenge was creating digital storage solutions that could handle large amounts of data. Today, with the advent of cloud computing and advanced data centers, the focus has shifted towards ensuring data privacy and security in an increasingly interconnected world.

Time does not just pass; it actively reshapes the problems we face, demanding adaptability and foresight in our problem-solving approaches.

The Sooner You Identify & Fix a Problem, the Simpler and Less Costly it Tends To Be

As a team of architects and engineers convened in the conference room, they stood on the cusp of a significant undertaking: the design of a skyscraper poised to transform the city's skyline. Aware that a project of this complexity would inevitably encounter challenges, they were committed to navigating them with precision.

In the nascent stages of design, they meticulously examined every facet of the building's structure, materials, and systems. Their pursuit of detail was exhaustive, aiming to pre-emptively address potential issues before they could morph into substantial complications.

Through comprehensive simulations, thorough analysis, and close collaboration, they laid a robust foundation for the project.

Despite rigorous planning, an unforeseen challenge surfaced: the original structural design, though aesthetically striking, was insufficient to bear the building's projected height and weight. The team realized the urgency of resolving this flaw to avert disastrous outcomes during construction.

With immediate effect, construction was paused, and specialist structural engineering consultants were enlisted to devise a solution. A revised framework meeting the necessary structural integrity criteria was soon established through meticulous redesign and reassessment.

The foresight to tackle this issue in the design phase was invaluable. Early detection prevented significant material wastage, labor losses, and construction delays. It also circumvented the need for extensive rework, helping the project adhere to its timeline and financial forecasts.

In the software development realm, teams abide by the adage "fail fast, fail forward." Leading complex projects, developers encounter myriad challenges, yet their agile approach enables early problem detection and resolution, keeping development costs in check.

The lesson is clear: the more protracted a problem becomes, the more complex and expensive its solution. Proactivity is thus financially astute.

Resolving Problems Quickly Is Crucial, But Preempting Them Is Even Better

This ethos directed the team's approach. Investing in the design phase allowed them to proactively confront challenges, averting potential delays and cost overruns, and preserving the structural integrity.

The episode underscored the importance of early problem detection and resolution in complex projects, showing that timely intervention during the planning stages simplifies processes and reduces expenses over the long haul.

As the project progressed, the lesson learned during the design phase became a guiding principle. The team's vigilance in anticipating and addressing problems early became the bedrock of their success, culminating in the creation of an architectural marvel destined to stand the test of time.

Neglecting early problem detection can have a compound effect, much like a persistent water drip. Initially, the droplets seem negligible, but over time, their cumulative effect is undeniable. Unaddressed issues, small at first, can expand into substantial obstacles, impeding progress and resource efficiency.

Unresolved problems, accumulating like unchecked water damage, can undermine structural integrity, sap resources, and thwart success. This analogy underscores the critical nature of timely problem identification and resolution. Ignoring even minor issues can lead to amplified and wide-ranging impacts over time.

Avoiding Complex Project Management Impacts

Traditional project management follows a meticulous path of planning and execution. Yet, when problems go unnoticed or unresolved, the resulting domino effect can reverberate across the project.

Initial issues, seemingly minor, can lead to reduced productivity as teams grapple with workarounds or temporary fixes. Efforts are diverted, efficiency drops, and timelines suffer. Rework becomes inevitable, as completed tasks require modifications to accommodate late solutions.

As deadlines are missed, costs escalate with the deployment of additional resources to tackle emerging issues. What might have been a manageable issue escalates into a complex tangle of challenges, disrupting productivity, increasing effort and rework, and straining the project budget.

This scenario serves as a stark reminder of the need for vigilance and proactive risk management in project management. Addressing issues at their inception is key to preventing a cascade of complications and maintaining project momentum, efficiency, and financial control.

Time vs. Money

The "Time vs. Money" principle in project management underscores the balance between speedy completion and adequate resourcing. The adage that "nine women cannot have a baby in one month" encapsulates the reality that certain tasks require a fixed amount of time, regardless of the resources thrown at them.

Acknowledging these inherent barriers—scientific laws, skilled personnel availability, task complexity—is fundamental.

No amount of money can expedite processes that are bound by these constraints. Project managers must balance resource allocation with realistic timelines to avoid inefficiencies, unnecessary costs, and the risk of project failure.

As projects extend over time, they become more susceptible to delays and cost overruns. The longer a project endures, the greater the potential for unforeseen hurdles and scope changes. Effective management of schedules and resources is paramount to preventing delays and controlling expenses.

Working Backwards in Time-Based Problems

Occasionally, project deadlines are immovable, necessitating a backward planning approach. Starting from the end goal, project managers map out milestones and tasks in reverse order to ensure alignment with the fixed deadline.

Consider organizing a large-scale music festival with a fixed opening day. The project manager, recognizing the need for reverse planning, starts by determining the final preparations—stage setup, sound systems, ticketing—then backtracks to earlier tasks such as vendor coordination and equipment procurement. This approach ensures each component is addressed in sequence, allowing for contingencies and final adjustments.

Working backwards offers several advantages: it clarifies priorities, streamlines resource management, and identifies potential bottlenecks, facilitating risk mitigation. It's an effective strategy for managing time-sensitive projects and ensuring on-time delivery.

Avoiding Timelines That Lead to Inadequate Solutions

It's crucial in project management to avoid deadlines that compromise the quality and functionality of deliverables. Rushing to meet timelines can result in products that only meet the bare minimum requirements, neglecting the project's long-term value and stakeholder satisfaction.

Prioritizing a balanced timeline that allows for high-quality deliverables is key to long-term success. Focusing solely on speed can force shortcuts and rushed decisions, while realistic timelines ensure that the project achieves its intended outcomes without sacrificing quality.

Businesses often have just one chance to impress customers and deliver excellence. This reality highlights the imperative to get it right the first time, as opportunities to correct shortcomings may be limited or nonexistent.

7.   The Nature of Problem-solving

Each problem possesses its unique characteristics and complexities, challenging the notion of a one-size-fits-all approach to problem-solving. Problem-solving encounters a diverse range of issues that defy rigid frameworks, emphasizing the need for creative and adaptive thinking.

Problems do not always conform to predefined structures or templates, requiring flexibility and adaptability in the problem-solving process. Therefore, problem-solving necessitates an open mindset that can transcend preconceived notions and embrace the fluidity and diversity of real-world challenges.

The nature of problem-solving is characterized by the need to navigate uncertainty, make informed decisions, and adapt strategies as new information emerges, ultimately leading to innovative solutions and personal growth.

The Need for Project Teams in Complex Problem-solving

As problems grow in scope, size, or complexity, the demand for collaborative problem-solving becomes apparent. There are challenges that surpass the abilities of a single individual. The formation of project teams is essential. Project teams bring together individuals with diverse skills, expertise, and perspectives to tackle complex problems.

By distributing the workload and leveraging the collective intelligence of team members, project teams can handle intricate tasks more effectively. The pooling of knowledge, experiences, and resources allows team members to approach the problem from various angles, promoting a comprehensive understanding and enabling innovative solutions.

Problem-solving is a complex endeavor that often requires a collective effort. While individual problem-solving skills are valuable, certain problems transcend the capabilities of a single person. This is where teams come into play.

The power of teamwork lies in the diversity of skills, perspectives, and experiences that each team member brings to the table. By pooling together their knowledge and expertise, teams can tackle multifaceted challenges more effectively and efficiently.

Furthermore, team members can support and complement each other, leveraging their unique strengths to find innovative solutions. The collaborative nature of teamwork fosters synergy, creativity, and a sense of collective ownership, ultimately leading to better problem-solving outcomes.

Interdisciplinary Teams

In some problem-solving scenarios, the complexity extends beyond a single field of expertise. This is where interdisciplinary teams become indispensable. An interdisciplinary team comprises individuals from different disciplines or fields who come together to address a problem collectively.

The benefit of interdisciplinary teams lies in their ability to provide a holistic perspective and consider various angles and dimensions of the problem at hand.

Combining diverse knowledge, skills, and approaches, interdisciplinary teams can overcome the limitations of a single-discipline focus and uncover novel solutions.

Additionally, these teams foster cross-pollination of ideas and promote learning among team members, leading to a richer problem-solving process. However, building and managing interdisciplinary teams can present unique challenges, such as communication barriers and conflicting viewpoints.

Therefore, it is crucial to establish effective communication channels, promote mutual respect, and encourage open-mindedness to harness the full potential of interdisciplinary problem-solving teams.

The collaborative nature of interdisciplinary teams provides not only increased problem-solving capacity but also fosters a sense of shared responsibility, accountability, and motivation, leading to higher levels of engagement and success in solving complex problems.

Example: Interdisciplinary Teams

In a project to revitalize a deteriorating urban neighborhood into a vibrant, sustainable community space, an interdisciplinary team is assembled.

This team includes urban planners, who bring expertise in efficient and sustainable city design; environmental scientists, focused on integrating eco-friendly practices; social workers, understanding community needs and fostering resident engagement; and architects, skilled in innovative, functional building designs.

The team is led by a project manager experienced in balancing diverse perspectives and driving collaborative projects to success.

The team collaborates intensively, with urban planners and architects working together to design public spaces that are both aesthetically pleasing and environmentally sustainable. Environmental scientists advise on green technologies and materials, ensuring the project's sustainability.

Social workers engage with the community, gathering input to ensure the project meets local needs and fosters a sense of ownership among residents.

Regular meetings, coupled with a dynamic, shared digital workspace, allow for ongoing communication and adjustment of plans, ensuring that the project remains responsive to both environmental goals and community needs.

This collaborative effort results in a transformed neighborhood that's not only sustainable but also deeply connected to the residents' aspirations and values.

The Fallacy of 'Thinking Out of the Box'

The concept of 'thinking out of the box' implies that there is a box—a set of assumptions, constraints, or predefined approaches—that restricts creative thinking. However, in reality, creative solutions emerge precisely when we challenge and transcend these assumed approaches or solutions.

Creativity thrives when we break free from conventional thinking patterns and explore new possibilities. It is not about thinking outside of a box, but rather about realizing that the box itself is an artificial construct that hampers our creativity.

True innovation arises from questioning assumptions, embracing ambiguity, and venturing into uncharted territories where we can discover unorthodox solutions.

All problems, regardless of their nature or complexity, lend themselves to starting with a 'blank sheet of paper.' This approach involves setting aside preconceived notions, biases, and established solutions, allowing for fresh and unrestricted thinking. By approaching a problem with a beginner's mind, we open ourselves up to new perspectives and possibilities.

Starting anew allows us to explore multiple angles, challenge existing assumptions, and consider alternative approaches that may have been overlooked. By discarding the constraints of previous solutions, we create space for unconventional ideas and novel insights to emerge.

Example: The Post-it Note

The concept of 'thinking out of the box' often suggests breaking away from conventional approaches or assumed constraints. However, the invention of the Post-it Note shows how innovation can stem from reassessing and reapplying existing ideas and materials, rather than discarding them in search of something entirely new.

In the late 1960s, Dr. Spencer Silver, a scientist at 3M, was attempting to develop a super-strong adhesive. Instead, he accidentally created a low-tack, reusable adhesive.

For years, this adhesive seemed like a failure; it didn't have an obvious use since it was weak compared to existing products. It didn't fit the 'box' of what an adhesive was supposed to be - strong and permanent.

Enter Art Fry, another 3M employee, who was frustrated that his bookmarks kept falling out of his hymnbook during choir practice.

Remembering Silver's adhesive, Fry had an out-of-the-box idea, but it wasn't about creating something entirely new. Instead, he thought of a new application for Silver's adhesive.

He coated it on paper, and the result was a bookmark that could stick to the pages without damaging them and was repositionable. This idea was the birth of the Post-it Note, which became one of 3M's most successful products.

This anecdote exemplifies that thinking out of the box isn't always about discarding existing ideas or looking for entirely new solutions.

Often, it's about looking at existing materials, ideas, or products from a new perspective and finding value in what might initially seem like a failure or a misfit.

Innovation often arises not by stepping outside of a familiar domain, but by reassessing and reimagining the potential of what's already there.

Overcoming Artificial Constraints and Unlocking Creativity

One of the challenges to unleashing creativity is the tendency for individuals to impose artificial constraints on themselves. These self-imposed 'boxes' limit our thinking and trap our creativity within predefined boundaries. Whether it's due to fear of failure, adherence to established norms, or a desire for quick and familiar solutions, we inadvertently confine our problem-solving capabilities.

Recognizing and breaking free from artificial constraints liberates our creativity. Embracing open-mindedness, embracing diverse perspectives, and reframing problems from different angles can help dismantle these self-imposed boxes and unlock the full potential of our creative thinking.

The Myth of "No Bad Ideas" in Brainstorming

Brainstorming sessions often promote the notion that there are no bad ideas, aiming to create an open and non-judgmental environment.

While this approach has its merits, it is important to recognize that not all ideas carry the same weight or contribute equally to the problem-solving process. Some ideas may lack feasibility, relevance, or practicality, and can potentially hinder progress or waste valuable time.

By perpetuating the belief that all ideas are equal, we run the risk of diluting the influence of genuinely good ideas that could lead to effective solutions. It is crucial to strike a balance between encouraging creativity and critical evaluation to identify and prioritize the most promising ideas.

Differentiating Between Valuable and Wasted Time

In the pursuit of inclusivity and avoiding potential hurt feelings, brainstorming sessions can sometimes descend into unproductive tangents or discussions that deviate from the core problem. While it is essential to create a supportive atmosphere, it is equally important to ensure that the collective time and energy of the group are utilized efficiently.

Recognizing the distinction between valuable contributions and ideas that may waste the group's time is crucial for maintaining focus and making progress.

By respectfully guiding the discussion and encouraging thoughtful participation, facilitators can help steer the brainstorming session towards fruitful outcomes while minimizing unproductive detours.

Balancing Creativity and Critical Evaluation

A successful brainstorming session strikes a balance between fostering creativity and incorporating critical evaluation. While it is important not to stifle creativity by immediately dismissing ideas, it is equally essential to evaluate and refine the generated ideas to filter out those with limited potential.

By introducing mechanisms for constructive feedback, refinement, and iteration, the group can harness the collective wisdom and enhance the quality of ideas.

Implementing evaluation criteria, such as feasibility, impact, and alignment with goals, helps ensure that the most promising ideas receive the attention and consideration they deserve, while still fostering an environment of collaboration and respect.

The Temptation of Using Old Solutions

When faced with a new problem, there is often a temptation to rely on familiar solutions that have been successful in the past. This inclination arises from a desire for efficiency, comfort, and the perception that if a solution worked previously, it should work again.

However, applying an old solution to a new problem can be misleading and potentially detrimental. Most problems are unique, characterized by their own set of complexities, nuances, and underlying factors.

While certain elements of previous solutions may be relevant, blindly applying them without considering the specifics of the new problem can lead to ineffective outcomes. It is essential to approach new problems with an open mind, recognizing the need for fresh perspectives and tailored approaches.

To effectively solve new problems, it is crucial to embrace adaptation and innovation rather than relying solely on old solutions. New challenges often require a departure from traditional thinking and a willingness to explore alternative paths.

This involves critically analyzing the unique aspects of the problem, understanding its root causes, and identifying key variables that may differ from previous situations.

By fostering a mindset of curiosity and experimentation, we can uncover novel solutions that address the specific needs of the new problem. Embracing adaptability and innovation allows us to break free from the limitations of preconceived solutions and tap into the full range of our problem-solving capabilities.

Embracing Mistakes as Learning Opportunities

In problem-solving, the mantra of "Be wrong – move on" emphasizes the importance of embracing mistakes as valuable learning opportunities. It acknowledges that not every attempt or solution will be successful, and that is perfectly acceptable. Instead of dwelling on failures or getting discouraged, this mindset encourages individuals to view mistakes as stepping stones toward progress.

By recognizing and reflecting upon our mistakes, we gain insights into what doesn't work, which can guide us towards more effective approaches.

This approach also encourages a growth mindset, fostering resilience, adaptability, and continuous improvement in the problem-solving process.

Embracing the philosophy of "Be wrong – move on" enables individuals to overcome fear of failure, embrace experimentation, and navigate the iterative nature of problem-solving.

In problem-solving, dwelling on mistakes or getting stuck in a cycle of self-doubt can hinder progress. The concept of "Be wrong – move on" emphasizes the significance of maintaining forward momentum. Instead of fixating on past failures, it encourages individuals to acknowledge the mistake, learn from it, and swiftly redirect their efforts towards finding alternative solutions.

This mindset helps prevent stagnation, fosters resilience, and preserves energy for future problem-solving endeavors. By swiftly moving on from errors, individuals can avoid getting trapped in unproductive cycles and maintain their focus on exploring new possibilities and approaches.

The ability to let go of past mistakes and keep moving forward is essential for sustained progress and eventual success in problem-solving.

Example: A Startup Pivot

Imagine a small tech startup, AlphaTech, which initially focused on developing a fitness tracking app. The team, driven by enthusiasm and market trends, invested significant time and resources into creating a feature-rich app.

However, upon launch, the app received lukewarm responses from users. The feedback pointed out that while the app was technically impressive, it was overly complicated and didn't effectively address specific user needs in the fitness tracking market.

Instead of seeing this as a failure, the CEO of AlphaTech, Alex, decided to use this as a learning opportunity. Alex convened the team for a series of meetings to analyze user feedback and review the app's performance. Through these discussions, it became clear that while their execution was flawed, the core technology they developed had potential.

The team realized that their strength lay not in creating consumer apps, but in the sophisticated data analysis algorithms they had developed. With this insight, AlphaTech pivoted. They repurposed their technology to create a B2B platform for health and fitness businesses, offering insights and analytics based on user data. This new direction leveraged their existing technology and addressed a clear market need that was not being met.

The pivot was a success. AlphaTech's new B2B platform quickly gained traction, with gyms and health centers appreciating the depth of insights provided.

The initial 'failure' of the fitness app was not the end, but a valuable stepping stone that led to a more successful and sustainable business model.

This experience ingrained in the AlphaTech team a culture of seeing mistakes as opportunities for growth and innovation, significantly contributing to their resilience and adaptability in a competitive tech industry.

8.   Some Problems Have Multiple Solutions

In the field of operations research, simplex equations form the backbone of solving complex optimization problems. These equations provide a systematic framework for finding the optimal solution in scenarios where resources must be allocated efficiently.

By representing the problem as a system of linear equations and inequalities, the simplex method explores a vast solution space. This method allows evaluating various feasible solutions at each iteration.

Through a series of pivoting and row operations, the algorithm navigates the constraints and variables, continuously improving the objective function value until the optimal solution is attained.

The beauty of simplex equations lies in their ability to address resource allocation problems with multiple constraints and competing objectives, enabling decision-makers to make informed choices that optimize efficiency and effectiveness.

The Iterative Essence of Problem-solving

Both problem-solving and the simplex method involve iterations and the evaluation of multiple options. Just as the simplex method systematically explores different combinations of variables, problem-solving often requires considering various approaches, ideas, or perspectives to find multiple solutions.

Emphasizing trade-offs is crucial in both simplex equations and problem-solving scenarios. In simplex equations, as the algorithm progresses from one solution to another, trade-offs emerge as variables are adjusted.

The algorithm strives to find the optimal solution by evaluating these trade-offs. Similarly, in problem-solving, multiple solutions often come with their own set of trade-offs, which can encompass factors like cost, time, feasibility, or effectiveness.

By carefully weighing these trade-offs, decision-makers can make informed choices and identify the most suitable solution. For instance, in a business context, a company may face the trade-off between investing in cutting-edge technology or allocating resources to improve customer service.

While investing in technology may enhance operational efficiency, it might come with a significant cost. Conversely, focusing on customer service might require allocating resources away from technology advancements.

By considering the trade-offs associated with each option, decision-makers can determine the optimal balance that aligns with the organization's goals and resources.

Trade-offs can illuminate the potential consequences of different choices and provide insights into the best course of action. When decision-makers weigh trade-offs, they gain a deeper understanding of the complexity involved in finding an optimal solution.

Considering the trade-offs in terms of cost, time, feasibility, and effectiveness, decision-makers can make well-informed decisions that maximize benefits and minimize drawbacks. In essence, emphasizing trade-offs empowers decision-makers to navigate the complexities of problem-solving and arrive at the most suitable solution for their specific context.

Factoring in Constraints

Exploring constraints and variables is fundamental in simplex equations, as they determine the feasibility and scope of possible solutions. Constraints restrict the values that variables can take, representing the limitations or requirements of a problem.

Variables, on the other hand, represent the unknowns or factors that can be adjusted to achieve the desired outcome. By manipulating constraints and variables within simplex equations, one can explore the range of feasible solutions and assess their viability.

This concept of constraints and variables can be directly applied to problem-solving in various domains. In real-world scenarios, constraints can be anything from budgetary limitations, and resource availability, to regulatory requirements and time constraints.

These constraints define the boundaries within which a solution must operate. Variables, on the other hand, represent the factors that can be adjusted or optimized to reach the desired outcome.

By carefully considering the constraints and variables in problem-solving, one can identify the factors that have the most significant impact on the solution space.

Adjusting or introducing different constraints and variables can have a profound effect on the potential solutions available. By relaxing or loosening certain constraints, new possibilities may emerge that were previously deemed unattainable.

Similarly, introducing new variables into the problem can open up additional avenues for exploration and innovation. For instance, in product development, adjusting the constraints of cost, time-to-market, and product features can lead to a range of different solutions.

By varying these factors, decision-makers can evaluate trade-offs and make informed choices that align with their objectives.

Sensitivity Analysis

Addressing sensitivity analysis is essential in both the simplex method and problem-solving processes. In the simplex method, sensitivity analysis evaluates how variations in the problem's parameters, such as coefficients or constraints, affect the optimal solution.

By systematically testing the sensitivity of the model, decision-makers can gain insights into the stability and reliability of the solution. Similarly, in problem-solving, sensitivity analysis involves examining how different factors or circumstances may impact the viability or desirability of potential solutions.

When conducting sensitivity analysis in problem-solving, decision-makers can assess how changes in external factors, market conditions, or resource availability influence the feasibility and effectiveness of different solutions.

Considering these variables, one can understand the robustness and adaptability of the proposed solutions under various scenarios.

For example, in a strategic business decision, sensitivity analysis can help determine how changes in customer demand, economic conditions, or competitive landscape may affect the success of different strategic options.

By addressing sensitivity analysis, decision-makers can better anticipate and plan for potential changes or uncertainties. Sensitivity analysis provides valuable insights into the flexibility and responsiveness of different solutions, allowing decision-makers to assess their resilience to external influences.

It enables them to identify potential risks, vulnerabilities, or opportunities associated with specific solutions and make informed decisions accordingly.

By understanding the sensitivity of solutions to various factors, decision-makers can optimize their choices and develop contingency plans to mitigate risks or seize opportunities that may arise in dynamic environments.

Ultimately, sensitivity analysis enhances the decision-making process by ensuring solutions are robust and adaptable in the face of changing circumstances.

Example: International Supply Chain

Imagine a company that relies on global suppliers for raw materials to manufacture its products. In this scenario, several factors can influence the viability and effectiveness of the supply chain. Conducting sensitivity analysis allows decision-makers to assess the impact of these factors on the supply chain's performance.

One crucial factor to consider in sensitivity analysis is exchange rates. Fluctuations in currency exchange rates can significantly affect the cost of imported raw materials.

By analyzing the sensitivity of the supply chain to exchange rate changes, decision-makers can assess how variations in currency values impact costs, profitability, and competitiveness. They can explore different scenarios by adjusting exchange rates and evaluate the financial implications on the supply chain's feasibility and profitability.

Another factor to consider is geopolitical stability. Political unrest, trade disputes, or regulatory changes in different countries can disrupt supply chains. Sensitivity analysis can help decision-makers understand how variations in geopolitical factors might affect the reliability and continuity of the supply chain.

Analyzing different scenarios, decision-makers can identify potential risks, develop contingency plans, or diversify suppliers to ensure the resilience and stability of the international supply chain.

Furthermore, sensitivity analysis can also encompass transportation costs and lead times. By assessing how variations in transportation costs, such as fuel prices or tariffs, impact the overall supply chain costs, decision-makers can identify cost-saving opportunities or alternative transportation routes.

Similarly, analyzing the sensitivity of lead times to factors like customs procedures or logistical disruptions helps decision-makers understand how variations in these variables influence production schedules and customer satisfaction.

In summary, sensitivity analysis for international supply chains involves assessing factors such as exchange rates, geopolitical stability, transportation costs, and lead times.

Analyzing the impact of these factors on the supply chain's performance, decision-makers can proactively identify risks, optimize costs, and develop strategies to enhance the resilience and effectiveness of the supply chain in an ever-changing global landscape.

Embracing Pragmatism: Moving Beyond the Search for Perfection

In the realm of problem-solving, it is essential to recognize that many problems have multiple good solutions. The pursuit of an ideal or perfect solution can sometimes be a trap, leading to excessive time, resources, and complexity. Instead, focusing on finding a good solution that provides ample benefits can be a pragmatic approach.

By carefully weighing the factors at play, such as cost, feasibility, and practicality, decision-makers can identify solutions that are not only effective but also efficient within the given constraints.

This mindset embraces the concept that there can be multiple paths to success, allowing for flexibility and adaptability in problem-solving processes.

Recognizing that the notion of an "ideal" solution is subjective and dependent on the context, the acceptance of multiple good solutions becomes crucial. What may be ideal in one scenario might not be feasible or practical in another. By broadening our perspective, we open ourselves up to alternative approaches and creative solutions.

Instead of striving for an unattainable perfection, the focus shifts towards finding solutions that strike a balance between different considerations. This pragmatic approach encourages decision-makers to assess trade-offs, consider the long-term implications, and ultimately make choices that optimize the available resources.

Embracing the notion of multiple good solutions is not a compromise or settling for mediocrity; rather, it is a strategic decision based on realistic constraints. By exploring various viable options, decision-makers can avoid getting stuck in analysis paralysis and achieve timely results.

This approach promotes efficiency, agility, and adaptability, as it recognizes that the value of a solution lies not only in its outcome but also in the resources invested to attain it.

Identifying and embracing multiple good solutions, decision-makers can effectively address problems, capitalize on opportunities, and make informed choices that align with their goals and constraints.

9. Some Problems Have No Solutions

In the realm of problem-solving, there exists a profound truth that can challenge our relentless pursuit of solutions. It is a truth that defies our most determined efforts and shatters our expectations: some problems simply do not have solutions.

This is the corollary to identifying multiple solutions for some problems. These enigmatic puzzles, like riddles without answers, leave us perplexed and contemplative.

No matter how diligently we search, how ardently we analyze, or how fervently we yearn for resolution, there are quandaries that elude the grasp of our problem-solving prowess. In this chapter, we delve into the realm of the unsolvable, embracing the paradoxical nature of these challenges and discovering the valuable lessons they hold for us.

Consider the heart-wrenching case of Emily, a vibrant and spirited woman in the prime of her life. Her world was abruptly shattered when she received the devastating diagnosis of an aggressive and incurable form of cancer.

In her quest for answers, Emily embarked on an arduous journey through countless medical consultations, second opinions, and experimental treatments. Her family and friends rallied around her, leaving no stone unturned in their collective pursuit of a solution.

Yet, despite their tireless efforts and unwavering hope, they soon came face to face with the harsh reality that some problems, like Emily's insidious cancer, defy the limits of our current medical knowledge. It was an agonizing realization that there was no definitive solution, no magic cure to be found.

This poignant example serves as a stark reminder that even the most fervent and sincere search for a solution may sometimes lead us to confront the stark truth: some problems remain unyielding, defying our most heartfelt desires for resolution.

Beyond the realm of health, the absence of solutions can cast its shadow upon various aspects of our lives. Imagine a small seaside town that has been grappling with a persistent environmental dilemma.

For years, its pristine beaches and crystal-clear waters have been plagued by an unrelenting onslaught of plastic waste, despite the community's best efforts to combat the problem.

Local activists, dedicated volunteers, and concerned citizens have joined forces, organizing beach clean-ups, implementing recycling programs, and advocating for stricter regulations. However, the tide of plastic seems unyielding, sweeping ashore with each passing day.

As the townspeople confront this ever-growing challenge, they come to a disheartening realization: some problems, like the relentless influx of plastic, may not have a clear-cut solution.

Their endeavors, while valiant, reveal the somber truth that certain problems extend beyond the boundaries of our immediate influence and demand a collective reassessment of our relationship with the environment.

Simultaneous Competing Deadlines

In the realm of productivity and time management, we often find ourselves entangled in a web of simultaneous competing deadlines. Picture this: you are a dedicated professional juggling multiple projects, each with its own set of pressing timelines.

As you meticulously plan your days, you realize that two critical deadlines loom overhead, demanding your attention and expertise.

The catch? These deadlines coincide, leaving you with an impossible choice. You possess the skills and resources to meet one deadline with precision, ensuring a job well done, but the price to pay is abandoning the other project, leaving it incomplete and potentially disappointing others who depend on your contributions.

The weight of such a dilemma can be paralyzing, highlighting the inescapable reality that, at times, the constraints of time force us to make tough decisions where one deadline triumphs while the other falls victim to circumstances beyond our control.

Simultaneous competing deadlines place us at the crossroads of ambition and compromise. They challenge our ability to prioritize, forcing us to confront our limitations and make peace with the fact that we cannot be everywhere at once. It becomes a delicate dance between meeting obligations and acknowledging our boundaries.

The art of navigating such a predicament lies in our capacity to evaluate the significance and impact of each deadline, assessing the consequences of our choices and communicating transparently with all parties involved.

While we may not possess the power to bend time to our will, we can embrace strategies such as effective delegation, collaboration, and open dialogue to mitigate the consequences of these competing demands.

This striking contrast of competing deadlines serves as a powerful reminder that in the intricate tapestry of problem-solving, even when solutions exist for each individual challenge, the convergence of conflicting demands can leave us grappling with the bitter truth that some problems, in their simultaneous nature, have no simultaneous solutions.

Being In Two Places At the Same Time

In the chaotic dance of our modern lives, there arises a perplexing challenge that defies the laws of physics and tests the boundaries of our existence: the need to be in two places at the same time.

We find ourselves caught between the relentless demands of personal and professional spheres, where obligations pull us in conflicting directions. As our calendars overflow with commitments, we face the daunting realization that our physical presence cannot be replicated, forcing us to confront the limitations of our mortal existence.

The desire to attend a crucial meeting while also being present for a loved one's important event, or the yearning to be at the forefront of two significant opportunities unfolding simultaneously, presents us with an inescapable quandary.

The longing to divide ourselves and stretch our presence across time and space embodies the essence of a dilemma where the convergence of aspirations and responsibilities reveals the inherent constraint that, as human beings, we are bound by the limits of our singular presence.

Imagine finding yourself entangled in a profound and emotionally charged predicament. Your best friend, with whom you have shared countless joys and sorrows, has chosen this very day to embark on a journey of love and commitment, as they walk down the aisle in a picturesque wedding ceremony.

Simultaneously, your next-door neighbor, a familiar face whose warmth and kindness have woven through the tapestry of your daily life, has tragically passed away, leaving behind a grieving family and community.

In this moment of deep human connection and conflicting responsibilities, you stand at the crossroads, grappling with an impossible choice.

Your heart yearns to celebrate the union of friendship and love, yet it also weighs heavy with the responsibility of paying final respects to a neighbor who has become an integral part of your small, tight-knit community.

It is in this poignant juxtaposition, the profound need to be in two places at the same time, that we confront the harsh reality that, despite our best intentions and fervent desires, we are bound by the limitations of our physical presence.

The unyielding demands of existence force us to make decisions that come at the cost of missing out on significant life events or foregoing opportunities to express our condolences, leaving us to grapple with the bittersweet realization that, at times, there is no perfect solution to the conundrum of being in two places at once.

The Solvable Problems

Within the vast landscape of human experiences, countless examples arise that illuminate problem domains where the quest for a single, universally satisfying solution proves to be a formidable challenge, if not an outright impossibility.

Amid the intricate tapestry of existence, we navigate a myriad of problem domains, each intricately woven with its own complexities and subtleties, where the elusive search for a solitary, universally satisfying solution is met with staunch resistance, compelling us to confront the inherent boundaries of our understanding and abilities.

For example:

- *Ethical Dilemmas*: Certain ethical quandaries, such as the classic "trolley problem," present complex scenarios where all choices have moral implications, and there is no clear solution that satisfies all ethical principles simultaneously.

- *Existential Questions*: The mysteries surrounding the purpose and meaning of life, the nature of consciousness, and the existence of a higher power are examples of profound questions that have perplexed humanity for centuries, often lacking definitive solutions.

- *Unsolved Mysteries*: In fields such as science, history, and crime. Examples include the enigma of dark matter, the identity of Jack the Ripper, or the fate of missing historical artifacts like the lost city of Atlantis.

- *Emotional Pain*: Some emotional challenges, such as grief, heartbreak, or the weight of past traumas, may not have a definitive solution. While coping strategies and healing processes can offer support, these experiences often require ongoing management rather than a single solution.

- *Philosophical Paradoxes*: Philosophical paradoxes, such as the Sorites Paradox or the Ship of Theseus, pose thought-provoking questions that challenge our understanding of logic, identity, and reality, often without clear-cut resolutions.

- *Social Conflicts*: In complex societal issues like political conflicts, cultural clashes, religious matters, or ideological debates, finding a universally agreed-upon solution is often elusive. These problems may involve deeply rooted beliefs, differing perspectives, and multifaceted dynamics that resist easy resolution.

Remember, each of these examples represents a problem domain where finding a single, universally satisfying solution can be challenging or even impossible.

10. Building Interdisciplinary Teams

In the realm of problem-solving, the power of collaboration knows no bounds. Throughout history, countless breakthroughs and monumental achievements have been accomplished by teams that bridge the boundaries of disciplines and bring together diverse perspectives.

When it comes to tackling complex challenges, one shining example that epitomizes the essence of interdisciplinary teamwork is NASA's Apollo program.

Launched amidst the space race of the 1960s, the Apollo program not only symbolized mankind's quest for the moon but also embodied the fusion of talent, expertise, and innovation from an array of companies and organizations.

As we delve into the intricacies of building interdisciplinary teams, we discover that the successful Apollo mission serves as a testament to the remarkable outcomes that can be achieved when individuals from different backgrounds unite their skills and knowledge towards a common goal.

In the pursuit of unprecedented goals, the Apollo program harnessed the collective power of individuals with diverse backgrounds in engineering, medicine, aeronautics, and the astronaut corps.

The engineering teams brought their technical prowess to design and construct the groundbreaking spacecraft, while medical professionals played a crucial role in ensuring the health and well-being of the astronauts throughout their space missions.

The field of aeronautics contributed its expertise in aviation and flight dynamics, guiding the intricate maneuvers necessary to navigate the vastness of space.

And let us not forget the brave astronauts themselves, whose rigorous training and unique understanding of the challenges inherent to space exploration made them the embodiment of interdisciplinary collaboration. These diverse backgrounds converged within the Apollo program, creating a rich tapestry of knowledge and skills that propelled humanity towards the stars.

Personalities Matter

In the realm of interdisciplinary teams, the value of expertise cannot be overstated. It is vital to assemble a team comprising individuals who possess the necessary skills and knowledge for the task at hand.

While technical competence is undoubtedly crucial, the diverse array of personalities within the group — an often underestimated aspect — significantly influences the team's dynamics and success.

Recognizing the importance of personalities within interdisciplinary teams goes beyond mere skill matching. It encompasses the need for a harmonious blend of individuals whose personalities complement and enhance each other's strengths, enabling effective collaboration.

> *Complementary Personalities*: Interdisciplinary teams thrive when individuals possess personalities that harmonize and complement each other. While it may be tempting to assemble a team of like-minded individuals, there is immense value in incorporating a range of personalities that offer varied perspectives and approaches.

> For instance, having individuals who are detail-oriented and meticulous alongside those who possess a big-picture thinking mindset can create a balance that leads to comprehensive problem-solving. Complementary personalities not only enhance creativity and innovation but also foster mutual support and synergy within the team.

> *Similar Personalities*: In certain scenarios, a team consisting of individuals with similar personalities can bring about a sense of cohesion and unity. Shared traits and characteristics can facilitate effective communication and understanding, streamlining decision-making processes. When team members possess a similar work ethic, drive, or motivation, it can create a cohesive environment where everyone is aligned towards a common goal.

> However, it is essential to ensure that there is still room for diversity within these shared personalities, as too much similarity can lead to groupthink or a lack of critical perspectives.

Divergent Personalities: On the other hand, embracing divergent personalities within interdisciplinary teams can yield remarkable results. When team members have contrasting perspectives, it encourages healthy debates, the exploration of multiple solutions, and the consideration of alternative viewpoints.

Diverse personalities can challenge conventional thinking, push boundaries, and foster innovation. By embracing the strengths and unique approaches of individuals with different personalities, interdisciplinary teams can tap into a broader range of ideas and problem-solving strategies.

In the realm of interdisciplinary teams, acknowledging the importance of personalities is paramount. While technical expertise serves as a prerequisite, the dynamics and effectiveness of the team are profoundly influenced by the blend of personalities within it.

By assembling a team that possesses a mix of complementary, similar, and divergent personalities, interdisciplinary teams can unlock the full potential of collaboration and problem-solving.

The art lies in finding the right balance, ensuring that personalities enhance each other's strengths while fostering an environment that values diversity and encourages open dialogue.

Effective management is crucial in building interdisciplinary teams and balancing the diversity of personalities within them. Skilled managers possess the ability to identify and leverage the strengths of individual team members, foster a collaborative environment, and facilitate productive communication, ensuring that the team's diverse personalities contribute to the overall success of the project.

Selecting Doer's vs. Thinkers in Interdisciplinary Teams

Building an effective interdisciplinary team involves careful consideration of the balance between individuals who excel at taking action and those who possess a penchant for deep thinking and conceptualization.

Understanding the roles of doers and thinkers within interdisciplinary teams and knowing when to include both or focus on one group is pivotal for maximizing the team's potential.

The Role of Doers: Doers are individuals who thrive in action-oriented roles, demonstrating a remarkable ability to execute tasks efficiently and effectively. They possess a practical mindset, excel at implementing plans, and are motivated by tangible results.

Doers are invaluable members of interdisciplinary teams, as they ensure that ideas are translated into concrete actions, tasks are completed, and progress is made. Their focus on implementation and execution drives the team forward, making them instrumental in turning concepts into reality.

The Role of Thinkers: Thinkers, on the other hand, are individuals who excel in the realm of ideation, conceptualization, and strategic thinking. They are inclined towards deep analysis, exploring different perspectives, and envisioning innovative solutions.

Thinkers have a knack for identifying patterns, understanding complex problems, and proposing creative approaches. They bring a critical and reflective mindset to the team, pushing for deeper understanding and guiding the team's direction through their intellectual insights.

Finding the Balance: While the roles of doers and thinkers may appear distinct, it is important to recognize that both are essential for the success of interdisciplinary teams. In some instances, a project may require a stronger focus on action and execution, necessitating a team predominantly comprised of doers.

Conversely, there are situations where the emphasis lies in exploring new ideas, developing strategies, and fostering innovation, making a team of thinkers more appropriate. However, striking the right balance often yields the best outcomes.

By including both doers and thinkers, teams can capitalize on the strengths of each group, enabling the practical implementation of thoughtful ideas and fostering a holistic approach to problem-solving.

In the realm of interdisciplinary teams, the selection of doers and thinkers is a critical aspect of team composition. Recognizing the distinct but complementary roles of these individuals is essential for achieving optimal results. By including individuals who excel at executing tasks alongside those who possess exceptional thinking abilities, teams can leverage the power of both action and innovation.

The key lies in understanding the nature of the project or problem at hand and determining whether a stronger focus on doers, thinkers, or a balanced combination is most appropriate. Through thoughtful selection, interdisciplinary teams can harness the strengths of doers and thinkers, maximizing their potential for success.

Being able to identify individuals or roles fitting these generalized categories is an essential skill for the management of large-complex projects.

The ability to strategically allocate the right mix of doers and thinkers based on the project's requirements ensures efficient execution and innovative problem-solving, ultimately contributing to the overall success of the endeavor.

Artistic vs. Technical – Both Can Be Creative

In the realm of interdisciplinary teams, it is essential to recognize that creativity is not confined to artistic disciplines alone. Each field, whether technical or artistic, possesses its own unique brand of creativity.

This underscores the notion that technical individuals can be highly creative in their own right, and conversely, artistic disciplines can exhibit precision and structure akin to engineering and scientific domains.

By appreciating the inherent creativity in all disciplines, we can foster a more holistic understanding of the diverse talents that contribute to interdisciplinary teams.

> *Creativity in Technical Disciplines*: Technical disciplines, often associated with precision and logic, also harbor immense creativity. Engineers, scientists, and other technical professionals engage in

creative problem-solving, innovation, and the design of intricate systems.

Their creativity lies in finding elegant and efficient solutions, optimizing processes, and pushing the boundaries of what is possible within the constraints of their fields. The marriage of creativity and technical expertise is exemplified by the well-known adage, "It's as much an art as it is a science," highlighting the artistry inherent in technical domains.

Precision and Structure in Artistic Disciplines: Conversely, artistic disciplines are often perceived as free-flowing and unstructured, but they can also exhibit remarkable precision and regimentation.

Artists, musicians, and other creatives dedicate themselves to honing their craft through disciplined practice, meticulous attention to detail, and adherence to established techniques and principles. They strive for excellence, embracing precision in their execution and striving to achieve their desired artistic vision.

This discipline within artistic domains resonates with the structured approach of engineers and scientists, showcasing the interconnectedness between artistry and precision.

Embracing the Diversity of Creative Expression: By recognizing that creativity exists across a broad spectrum of disciplines, interdisciplinary teams can harness the power of diverse perspectives and talents. Artistic and technical individuals bring unique creative strengths to the table, fostering innovation and fostering dynamic problem-solving.

Embracing the diversity of creative expression within interdisciplinary teams allows for a richer exchange of ideas, leading to novel approaches and holistic solutions.

In the world of interdisciplinary teams, it is essential to acknowledge the creativity present in both artistic and technical disciplines. Technical fields demonstrate their own form of creativity through innovative problem-solving and design, while artistic disciplines exhibit precision and structure in pursuit of artistic excellence.

By embracing the diversity of creative expression across disciplines, interdisciplinary teams can tap into a wealth of perspectives and talents, leading to more comprehensive and imaginative solutions.

Appreciating the interconnectedness of artistry and precision promotes a collaborative environment where all team members' unique creative contributions are valued.

Some Teams Can Thrive on Conflict

While conflict is often seen as detrimental to teamwork, it is important to recognize that certain teams can thrive in the presence of conflict. When managed effectively, conflict can fuel innovation, enhance problem-solving, and foster a deeper understanding among team members. Conflict can be a catalyst for growth within interdisciplinary teams and can lead to improved outcomes and team dynamics.

> *Stimulating Innovation and Creativity*: Conflict within interdisciplinary teams can serve as a catalyst for stimulating innovation and creativity. Differing viewpoints, opinions, and approaches can ignite spirited debates that challenge conventional thinking and push the boundaries of problem-solving.
>
> Through constructive conflict, team members are encouraged to question assumptions, explore alternative perspectives, and propose innovative solutions. The clash of ideas can inspire new ways of thinking, leading to breakthroughs and novel approaches that may not have been considered in the absence of conflict.
>
> *Enhancing Collaboration and Understanding*: Conflict, when managed effectively, can enhance collaboration and deepen understanding among team members. Through respectful and open discussions, conflicts allow individuals to articulate their viewpoints, express concerns, and share diverse experiences.
>
> By actively listening and engaging in constructive dialogue, team members develop a deeper understanding of one another's perspectives and insights. This enhanced understanding fosters empathy, empathy, and builds trust within the team, creating a foundation for stronger collaboration and synergy.

Consider a research and development team tasked with developing cutting-edge technology solutions. In this team, diverse perspectives and expertise are essential for driving innovation. During the brainstorming and decision-making processes, team members engage in healthy debates and constructive conflicts.

Varied opinions, technical expertise, and creative ideas clash, leading to in-depth discussions and critical evaluations of different approaches. By embracing conflict as a means of challenging assumptions and exploring alternative solutions, the team fosters an environment where innovative ideas flourish.

The outcome is a series of breakthrough technological advancements that wouldn't have been possible without the productive conflicts that fueled the team's creativity and problem-solving capabilities.

While conflict is often viewed negatively, certain teams can thrive when conflict is managed effectively. Productive conflict can stimulate innovation, enhance problem-solving, and foster deeper collaboration and understanding among team members.

By embracing conflict as a catalyst for growth, interdisciplinary teams can harness the diverse perspectives and ideas of their members, leading to improved outcomes, stronger team dynamics, and ultimately, greater success.

Leadership in Building Large Interdisciplinary Teams

When building large interdisciplinary teams, it is crucial to have effective leadership in place. While group management may seem appealing, it is essential to recognize that someone needs to be in charge to ensure coordination, decision-making, and overall team success.

The selected leader must possess the ability to listen to and incorporate the input of individuals from various disciplines, fostering a collaborative and inclusive environment.

In large interdisciplinary teams, having a designated leader with clear coordination and decision making skills is essential. The leader assumes the responsibility of aligning team objectives, setting priorities, and ensuring that the team operates cohesively towards a common goal.

With a clear chain of command, team members can rely on the leader for guidance, direction, and timely decision-making, promoting efficiency and progress within the team.

An effective leader in large interdisciplinary teams must also possess strong listening skills and an inclusive leadership style. Recognizing the diverse perspectives and expertise within the team, the leader must actively seek input from individuals across disciplines, encouraging open dialogue and valuing contributions from all team members.

By creating a safe and inclusive space for collaboration, the leader ensures that diverse ideas are heard and respected, leading to better decision-making and the utilization of the collective intelligence of the team.

One of the key roles of a leader in large interdisciplinary teams is to bridge the divides between different disciplines. By facilitating communication and understanding among team members from various backgrounds, the leader fosters a sense of unity and shared purpose.

This helps overcome potential conflicts and encourages the integration of different perspectives and expertise, leading to a more comprehensive and holistic approach to problem-solving.

Effective leadership is paramount for the success of large interdisciplinary teams. Selecting a leader with requisite skills and confident decision-making builds unity among a diverse team.

An attentive and inclusive leadership style, marked by active listening and valuing input from all disciplines, cultivates collaboration and harnesses the collective intelligence of the team.

By bridging disciplinary gaps, the leader facilitates the harmonious integration of diverse perspectives and expertise. The selection of suitable leadership for large interdisciplinary teams lays the foundation for fruitful collaboration, innovative problem-solving, and, ultimately, the attainment of team objectives.

11. Solving For Grey

In the realm of problem-solving, it is crucial to recognize that not all dilemmas can be neatly categorized into black and white, yes or no, or right and wrong.

Life is often filled with complex situations that demand a more nuanced approach. These are the instances where we encounter the shades of grey, where the lines blur and the solutions become more elusive.

Instead of seeking simple, binary answers, we must embrace the notion that some problems require a different kind of thinking—one that appreciates the intricacies, uncertainties, and multiple perspectives at play. Solving for grey invites us to step beyond the confines of rigid dichotomies and explore the vast spectrum of possibilities.

When confronted with problems that defy simplistic categorization, the true power of problem-solving lies in our ability to navigate the grey areas.

Such situations often call for creative thinking, critical analysis, and a willingness to embrace ambiguity. Solving for grey demands that we expand our toolkit of strategies and consider a wider range of options.

It requires us to explore the middle ground, seek compromises, and find novel approaches that can address the complexities inherent in these challenges.

By understanding that not all problems have clear-cut solutions, we open ourselves up to the potential for innovative and transformative problem-solving, paving the way for progress in both personal and professional spheres.

Addressing Missing or Undefined Factors

One of the inherent complexities of problem-solving is encountering situations where critical factors are missing or undefined. It is in these moments of uncertainty that our problem-solving skills are truly put to the test. When faced with incomplete information or unaccounted variables, we must adopt a proactive and adaptable mindset. Rather than being deterred by the absence of clarity, we can view it as an opportunity to delve deeper, conduct thorough investigations, and uncover hidden insights.

Solving problems with missing or undefined factors demands a willingness to embrace ambiguity, employ creative thinking, and engage in robust analysis to identify the underlying patterns and relationships that can shed light on the elusive aspects of the problem.

The presence of missing or undefined factors in a problem requires us to approach problem-solving with a degree of humility. We must acknowledge that our initial assumptions or preconceived notions may not hold true in the face of incomplete information. This necessitates a commitment to continuous learning and adaptation throughout the problem-solving process.

Rather than hastily jumping to conclusions or relying on limited data, we must invest time and effort into gathering more information, consulting experts, or conducting experiments to gain a deeper understanding of the problem.

In some cases modeling of problems can lead an acceptable solution or present a basis for choosing among seemingly similar good options.

Imagine a city called Riverton, which is experiencing rapid population growth and severe traffic congestion on its existing roads. The city council decides to address this issue by constructing a new highway to alleviate the traffic burden. However, they face a crucial question: "How many people will use the new highway daily?"

To answer this question, the council hires an engineering company that considers various factors, including the existing regional traffic patterns and the anticipated future growth of the surrounding areas.

However, they soon realize that predicting the exact number of daily users is challenging due to several undefined factors. For instance, they need to account for potential changes in commuting patterns, the impact of urban development projects, and shifts in population density.

Moreover, there are unpredictable variables, such as the future adoption of electric or autonomous vehicles, changes in public transportation systems, or the emergence of alternative commuting options.

There is also the long-term impact of work-from-home trends. All these factors contribute to the uncertainty surrounding the estimation of daily highway usage or even whether the long-term assumptions may be valid.

As a result, the engineering company recognizes that they need to conduct in-depth research, collaborate with traffic experts, analyze historical data, and consider various growth scenarios to obtain a more accurate estimation.

They understand that the success of the new highway project depends on accounting for these undefined factors and making informed decisions based on the best available information.

This example illustrates how the construction of a new highway in a growing and traffic-congested region introduces undefined factors that make it challenging to determine the exact number of daily users.

It emphasizes the importance of thorough research, collaboration, and adaptability in addressing such uncertainties during the problem-solving process.

Educated Guesses

In the realm of problem-solving, there are instances where certain factors are either unknown or deemed unknowable.

When faced with such uncertainty, making educated guesses becomes an invaluable skill. It relies on our understanding of the problem domain, drawing upon our experience, knowledge, and intuition to navigate through the fog of uncertainty.

Educated guessing is not a haphazard or random approach. Rather, it involves a thoughtful analysis of the available information, careful consideration of patterns and trends, and leveraging our expertise to make informed predictions or assumptions.

It is a process that combines logic, reasoning, and creativity, allowing us to fill in the gaps and take calculated risks in pursuit of finding effective solutions to complex problems.

Making educated guesses requires a deep familiarity with the problem at hand and the ability to identify relevant patterns and indicators that can guide our decision-making. It involves drawing upon our accumulated knowledge, previous experiences, and even insights gained from analogous situations.

Through a combination of critical thinking, analysis, and intuition, we can make informed estimates or projections, taking into account the known variables and their potential influence on the unknown or unknowable factors.

While there may be inherent risks involved in relying on educated guesses, they serve as valuable stepping stones that help us move forward, adapt our strategies, and gain further clarity as we gather more information.

Educated guessing is a testament to the power of our cognitive abilities and experience in navigating the complex landscape of problem-solving.

Applying Artificial Intelligence

The emergence of artificial intelligence (AI) holds immense promise in revolutionizing problem-solving, particularly when dealing with unknown factors. AI systems have the capacity to analyze vast amounts of data, detect intricate patterns, and uncover hidden insights that may elude human intuition alone.

By training AI models on diverse datasets and leveraging advanced algorithms, we can harness the power of machine learning to bridge the gaps associated with unknown factors. AI algorithms can simulate scenarios, conduct complex simulations, and generate probabilistic predictions based on a multitude of variables and potential outcomes.

This not only aids in generating more accurate educated guesses but also expands our understanding of the problem domain by revealing new perspectives and previously unrecognized relationships.

As AI technologies continue to advance, we can envision a future where problem-solving becomes a collaborative process between human expertise and AI-driven insights, significantly improving our ability to tackle complex challenges with precision and confidence.

The integration of AI into problem-solving has the potential to unlock new levels of accuracy and efficiency in making educated guesses.

AI algorithms excel at processing and analyzing vast amounts of data, quickly identifying relevant patterns and correlations that might elude human observers.

By leveraging these capabilities, AI can help bridge the gaps associated with unknown factors, enhancing the accuracy of our guesses and predictions.

Additionally, AI systems can continuously learn and adapt through iterative processes, refining their models based on real-time feedback and new information.

As a result, AI-powered problem-solving becomes an iterative and dynamic process, with the potential to continually improve and deliver increasingly accurate educated guesses.

While human judgment and expertise remain indispensable, the integration of AI in problem-solving with unknown factors opens up exciting possibilities for more informed decision-making and innovative solutions.

Bringing Clarity to Ambiguous Goals and Objectives

Clear and well-defined goals or objectives are the cornerstone of successful project completion. When faced with poorly defined goals, it is all too common for individuals or teams to be directed to hastily complete projects without a clear understanding of what is truly expected.

This lack of clarity or specificity often leads to suboptimal results and outcomes that run counter to the intended purpose.

Without a clear destination in mind, it becomes challenging to navigate the path effectively, resulting in wasted efforts, misaligned priorities, and dissatisfaction among stakeholders.

To address this issue, it is essential to recognize the importance of clarifying poorly defined goals or objectives – early in the process!

By taking the time to clearly articulate and communicate the desired outcomes, individuals and teams can align their efforts, make informed decisions, and work towards a shared vision, thereby increasing the likelihood of achieving success.

Clarity in goals or objectives serves as a guiding light throughout the project lifecycle. It provides a framework for decision-making, resource allocation, and progress evaluation. When goals lack specificity, ambiguity creeps in, leading to misunderstandings, misinterpretations, and ultimately, a divergence from the desired outcomes.

Clear and well-defined goals, on the other hand, enable individuals and teams to prioritize tasks, set realistic timelines, and allocate resources effectively.

They foster a sense of purpose and direction, empowering stakeholders to make informed choices, overcome obstacles, and adapt strategies as needed.

By proactively seeking clarity in poorly defined goals or objectives, organizations can foster a culture of transparency, alignment, and accountability, which lays the foundation for successful project execution and the attainment of desired results.

Unpredictability of Customer Expectations

The unpredictability of customer expectations poses a significant challenge for businesses and organizations across various domains. The truth is, many customers have limited knowledge or a vague idea of what they truly want.

Whether it's a new product, a proposed solution, or a poorly understood objective, customers can be their own worst enemy and inadvertently create obstacles.

With unclear objectives, they may struggle to articulate their needs or provide definitive requirements, making it difficult for businesses to meet their expectations.

This unpredictability forces companies to navigate a complex landscape, requiring them to employ agile and adaptable strategies.

By adopting a customer-centric approach that emphasizes active listening, proactive communication, and iterative feedback, businesses can better understand and respond to the ever-changing expectations of customers, fostering strong relationships and delivering more successful outcomes.

Customers with poorly understood objectives often become a challenging aspect of the business landscape by consistently "moving the goal posts."

As the discovery process unfolds and businesses strive to fulfill customer requirements, there can be a tendency for customers to revise their expectations or introduce new criteria.

This shifting landscape can frustrate organizations that have invested time and resources in meeting the initially defined objectives.

The continuous movement of the goal posts can lead to delays, scope creep, and potential dissatisfaction on both sides. To mitigate this challenge, open and transparent communication is essential.

Sometimes, amidst the complexities of customer demands and ever-evolving requirements, the simplest and most effective approach is to define the objectives for the customer.

While customers may struggle to articulate their precise needs or have ambiguous expectations, businesses can play a pivotal role in guiding the process by proactively collaborating with customers to establish clear and well-defined objectives.

By leveraging their expertise and understanding of the industry landscape, businesses can help customers clarify their goals, align their vision, and set achievable targets.

Defining the objectives not only brings clarity to the project but also ensures that efforts are focused and resources are allocated efficiently, leading to a more successful outcome that meets or exceeds the customer's expectations.

But as a general rule, businesses should proactively engage with customers, seek clarity, and manage expectations through clear documentation and regular checkpoints.

Additionally, fostering a collaborative partnership with customers and involving them in the decision-making process can help align objectives and minimize the effects of constantly shifting expectations.

Why Specifications Can Be Good

Specifications play a vital role in ensuring clarity, consistency, and successful outcomes in various endeavors. By clearly defining the requirements, parameters, and desired outcomes, specifications provide a shared understanding among stakeholders, whether it's in product development, project management, or any other domain.

They serve as a roadmap, guiding the process and enabling effective communication between teams and clients. Specifications help set clear expectations, providing a framework for decision-making, resource allocation, and progress evaluation.

They promote accountability, as teams can refer to the specifications to ensure they are meeting the agreed-upon criteria. Moreover, specifications allow for more efficient collaboration, as they help identify potential issues, prevent misunderstandings, and facilitate timely adjustments.

Ultimately, well-crafted specifications contribute to improved project outcomes, reduced risks, and enhanced customer satisfaction.

In addition to providing clarity and direction, specifications can also foster innovation and creativity. While some may perceive specifications as restrictive or limiting, they can actually inspire creative problem-solving within the defined boundaries.

Specifications act as a challenge, encouraging teams to think outside the box and find innovative solutions within the given constraints.

When well-crafted, specifications define the problem space and its limitations, enabling teams to explore different approaches, experiment with ideas, and push the boundaries of what is possible.

By delineating the core requirements, specifications help teams focus their efforts and resources on finding inventive ways to meet those requirements.

Consequently, specifications can serve as a catalyst for breakthrough thinking, driving teams to develop unique and value-added solutions that meet or exceed the specified criteria.

12. Applying Logic

Logic serves as a fundamental tool in the realm of problem-solving, providing a structured framework for reasoning and analysis. By understanding the general concepts of logic, individuals can develop a systematic approach to address complex issues.

Logic aids in identifying and evaluating the relationships between different elements within a problem, enabling the formulation of logical arguments and deductions. Through logical reasoning, problem solvers can break down intricate problems into manageable components and discern patterns or connections that may not be immediately apparent.

By applying logical thinking, they can draw conclusions based on evidence, identify potential gaps in information, and construct coherent solutions. The application of logic to problem-solving helps to enhance critical thinking skills and fosters a methodical approach that promotes effective decision-making.

Deductive vs. Inductive Reasoning

When employing logic in problem-solving, individuals often encounter two distinct modes of reasoning: deductive and inductive.

Deductive reasoning involves drawing specific conclusions based on established premises or general principles. It follows a top-down approach, moving from general statements to specific implications.

Deductive reasoning allows problem solvers to derive logical consequences from known information, enabling them to make precise predictions or reach definitive solutions.

On the other hand, inductive reasoning takes an opposite approach, working from specific observations or data to form generalizations or theories.

Inductive reasoning allows problem solvers to identify patterns or trends based on empirical evidence, facilitating the formulation of hypotheses or probable solutions. Both deductive and inductive reasoning play crucial roles in problem-solving, providing complementary methods that expand the range of strategies available to individuals as they tackle various types of problems.

<u>Example of deductive reasoning</u>

Premise 1: All mammals are warm-blooded animals.

Premise 2: A whale is a mammal.

Conclusion: Therefore, a whale is a warm-blooded animal.

In this example, deductive reasoning is employed to draw a specific conclusion based on established premises. By using the general statement that all mammals are warm-blooded animals (Premise 1) and the specific information that a whale is a mammal (Premise 2), we can deduce the conclusion that the whale is a warm-blooded animal.

<u>Example of inductive reasoning</u>:

Observation 1: Every time John eats peanuts, he develops an allergic reaction.

Observation 2: Every time Sarah eats peanuts, she develops an allergic reaction.

Observation 3: Every time Emily eats peanuts, she develops an allergic reaction.

Conclusion: Therefore, it is likely that peanuts cause allergic reactions in some people.

In this example, inductive reasoning is used to form a generalization or theory based on specific observations. The repeated instances of individuals experiencing allergic reactions after consuming peanuts lead to the conclusion that peanuts are likely to cause allergic reactions in some people. Inductive reasoning allows us to make probable conclusions or predictions based on patterns or trends observed in specific cases.

These examples illustrate how deductive reasoning involves deriving specific conclusions from general principles, while inductive reasoning involves forming generalizations or theories based on specific observations or data.

Predicate vs. Aristotelian

Predicate logic and Aristotelian logic are two distinct systems of formal logic that have different approaches to representing and analyzing logical relationships.

Predicate logic, also known as first-order logic, extends traditional propositional logic by introducing quantifiers and predicates. It allows for the representation of complex relationships between objects or individuals.

In predicate logic, variables are used to represent objects or individuals, and predicates are used to describe properties or relationships. Quantifiers such as "for all" ($\forall$) and "there exists" ($\exists$) are employed to express statements about all or some objects within a given domain.

Predicate logic provides a more expressive and precise language for logical reasoning, enabling the analysis of intricate relationships and the formulation of sophisticated arguments.

Aristotelian logic, also referred to as traditional logic, is based on the work of the ancient Greek philosopher Aristotle. It focuses on categorizing and analyzing statements in terms of their logical form and the relationships between terms.

Aristotelian logic is a way of thinking that focuses on statements about groups or types of things. These statements are called categorical propositions, and they make claims about different categories or classes of objects. In these propositions, we have different parts like subjects and predicates, which are connected using words like "is" or "is not."

Aristotelian logic is interested in the qualities (positive or negative) and quantities (whether they apply to everything or only some things) of these statements. It uses a method called syllogism to draw conclusions based on these categorical propositions.

This way of thinking provides a structured approach to understanding how different groups or categories are related to each other, and it has played a crucial role in the development of logic as a field of study.

Theory, Axioms, and Theorems

The concepts of theory, axioms, and theorems are fundamental elements in logic and mathematics, and they have wide-ranging applications in various disciplines.

By applying theories, leveraging axioms, and utilizing proven theorems, professionals in various fields can approach problems with a systematic and logical mindset, leading to more effective problem-solving strategies and solutions.

A theory provides a framework for studying a subject area, axioms are the foundational assumptions within that framework, and theorems are the proven statements derived from those axioms and other established principles.

Theories encompass broader areas of knowledge, while axioms and theorems are specific elements within a theory that contribute to its logical structure and enable rigorous reasoning and proof.

A theory is a systematic framework that explains and predicts phenomena within a specific domain. It consists of fundamental concepts, definitions, assumptions, and laws that form the basis for understanding and studying a subject area. Theories provide a comprehensive framework for organizing knowledge and making predictions.

In engineering, theories provide the conceptual frameworks for understanding and designing complex systems, such as electrical circuits, structural mechanics, or fluid dynamics.

> *Example*: The theory of relativity, formulated by Albert Einstein, provides a framework for understanding the behavior of space, time, and gravity. It includes concepts such as the equivalence of mass and energy ($E=mc^2$) and the bending of spacetime by massive objects. The theory of relativity allows us to make predictions

about the behavior of objects in extreme gravitational fields, such as the bending of starlight around a massive object.

An axiom, also known as a postulate, is a self-evident truth or a basic principle that is accepted without proof within a logical or mathematical system. Axioms serve as foundational assumptions upon which logical or mathematical reasoning is built. They establish the rules of inference and logical structure within a specific context.

Axioms form the foundational principles in fields like computer science and programming, establishing the logical rules and assumptions for building robust algorithms and software.

Example: In Euclidean geometry, one of the fundamental axioms is the parallel postulate, which states that given a line and a point not on that line, there exists exactly one line through the point that is parallel to the given line.

This axiom, along with other axioms, forms the foundation of Euclidean geometry and allows us to reason about parallel lines, angles, and shapes in a two-dimensional space.

A theorem is a statement that has been proven to be true within a logical or mathematical system based on established axioms, definitions, and other theorems.

Theorems are derived through rigorous logical reasoning and proof techniques. They represent the formal outcomes of deductive reasoning and provide valuable insights or solutions within a particular theory.

Theorems, derived through rigorous mathematical proofs, are essential in fields such as physics, where they help describe the behavior of particles and phenomena.

Moreover, these logical elements play a crucial role in problem-solving across diverse domains, including business disciplines such as operations research, economics, and decision analysis.

Example: Pythagoras' theorem states that in a right-angled triangle, the square of the length of the hypotenuse (the side opposite the right angle) is equal to the sum of the squares of the lengths of the other two sides.

This theorem, proven using deductive reasoning from Euclidean geometry axioms, has wide-ranging applications in various fields, such as architecture, engineering, and physics, and helps us calculate unknown sides or angles in right-angled triangles.

Logical Elements for Reasoning and Analysis

There are logic elements that provide tools for reasoning about various aspects of propositions, relationships, and conditions. By understanding these concepts, one can navigate and analyze logical structures more effectively.

Identity: Identity refers to the concept of being the same or equivalent. In logic, identity is denoted by the symbol "=" and is used to assert that two objects or terms refer to the same thing. For example, in the statement "A = B," we assert that the objects represented by A and B are identical or indistinguishable.

Truth: Truth in logic pertains to the correspondence between a statement and reality. In logical reasoning, a proposition or statement can be evaluated as either true or false. The truth value of a statement depends on whether it accurately reflects the state of affairs or conforms to the facts.

Quantification: Quantification involves expressing the extent or scope of a statement. In logic, quantifiers such as "forall" ($\forall$) and "exists" ($\exists$) are used to indicate the quantity of objects that satisfy a given condition. The universal quantifier ($\forall$) asserts that a statement is true for all objects in a particular domain, while the existential quantifier ($\exists$) asserts that at least one object exists that satisfies the given condition.

Existence: Existence refers to the state of being or the presence of something. In logic, the existential quantifier ($\exists$) is used to assert that at least one object exists that satisfies a given condition. It acknowledges the presence of an object or entity that meets the specified criteria.

Entailment: Entailment denotes a logical relationship between two statements where one statement logically follows or is a necessary consequence of another. If statement A entails statement B, it means that whenever statement A is true, statement B must also be true.

Modality: Modality in logic pertains to expressing possibility, necessity, or impossibility. Modal logic introduces modal operators such as "necessarily" ($\Box$) and "possibly" ($\Diamond$) to specify the modal status of a statement. These operators allow us to reason about what is necessarily true, possible, or impossible.

Necessity: Necessity refers to the requirement or inevitability of something being true. In modal logic, the operator "necessarily" ($\Box$) is used to indicate that a statement must be true in all possible worlds or under all possible conditions.

Decision Trees, Branching Logic and Decision Making

Decision trees are graphical representations that depict a sequence of decisions and their potential outcomes in a structured manner. They serve as powerful tools for decision analysis and problem-solving.

A decision tree starts with an initial decision or question and branches out into various possible choices or paths based on different conditions or criteria.

Each branch represents a decision point, leading to subsequent branches or leaves that signify the potential outcomes or actions associated with each choice. By following the branches of a decision tree, individuals can systematically analyze the available options, evaluate the associated risks or rewards, and make informed decisions based on the anticipated outcomes.

Decision trees provide a visual framework for understanding complex decision-making processes, enabling individuals to identify the most optimal path or course of action for a given situation.

Branching logic refers to the logical structure or rules used to determine the flow of decisions and actions within a system or process. It involves defining conditional statements or rules that determine which branch or path to follow based on specific conditions or criteria.

Branching logic is commonly used in computer programming, survey design, and business rule systems to handle different scenarios or outcomes. It allows for the creation of dynamic decision-making processes where the subsequent steps or choices are dependent on the outcomes of previous decisions or the evaluation of certain conditions.

By incorporating branching logic, systems can adapt and respond intelligently to different inputs or circumstances, leading to more tailored and effective decision-making.

Effective decision making involves utilizing decision trees and branching logic to systematically evaluate options, consider relevant factors, and choose the most favorable course of action. By employing decision trees, individuals can visualize the decision-making process, identify key decision points, and consider the potential consequences of their choices.

Branching logic helps determine the flow of decisions and actions based on specific conditions or criteria, ensuring that the decision-making process is flexible and responsive to changing circumstances. Together, decision trees and branching logic provide valuable tools for structuring, analyzing, and optimizing decision-making processes across various domains and contexts.

The Laws of Thought

The laws of thought form the bedrock of classical logic, providing foundational principles that govern rational thinking and reasoning. Traditionally, three fundamental laws of logic have been recognized: the law of contradiction, the law of excluded middle (or third), and the principle of identity.

The law of contradiction states that a proposition cannot be both true and false simultaneously. In other words, contradictory statements cannot be true in the same sense and at the same time.

For instance, the proposition "It is raining" and its negation "It is not raining" cannot both be true simultaneously. The law of contradiction ensures logical consistency by prohibiting contradictory claims from being simultaneously affirmed.

The law of excluded middle (or third) asserts that for any given proposition, it must either be true or its negation must be true. There is no middle ground or third option.

For example, when considering the proposition "The coin will land heads up," according to the law of excluded middle, it is either true that the coin will land heads up or true that it will not land heads up. The law of excluded middle ensures that every proposition has a definite truth value, either true or false.

The principle of identity states that a thing is the same as itself, or in other words, any statement of the form "A is A" is necessarily true. This principle is grounded in the concept of individuality and uniqueness.

For example, the statement "The Eiffel Tower is the Eiffel Tower" is an instance of the principle of identity. It reaffirms the self-identity and non-contradictory nature of an object or concept.

These laws of thought serve as fundamental principles of logic, guiding the principles of reasoning and inference. They provide the logical framework for coherent thinking and analysis, ensuring consistency and validity in logical arguments and deductions.

By adhering to these laws, one can avoid contradictions, classify propositions as true or false, and affirm the identity and non-contradictory nature of objects and concepts in logical discourse.

Converting Problems to a Series of Binary Answers

Applying logic to problem-solving often involves breaking down complex problems into a series of binary or discrete steps. By decomposing a problem into smaller, more manageable components, individuals can systematically analyze and tackle each step using logical reasoning.

This approach allows problem solvers to approach the problem in a structured manner, reducing ambiguity and facilitating a clearer understanding of the underlying issues.

Breaking down the problem into discrete steps helps identify dependencies, relationships, and potential bottlenecks, enabling a more targeted and efficient problem-solving process.

Converting problems into a series of binary or discrete steps enables problem solvers to employ logical thinking and decision-making at each stage. Each step represents a clear decision point or action to be taken, allowing for systematic evaluation and selection of the most appropriate course of action.

By applying logical reasoning, problem solvers can assess the available information, analyze cause-and-effect relationships, consider alternative solutions, and make informed decisions based on evidence and logical inference.

This structured approach enhances problem-solving capabilities by eliminating guesswork and providing a well-defined path to follow, leading to more effective and efficient problem resolution.

Weighting Decision Points

In problem-solving and decision-making processes, it is crucial to recognize that not all decision points carry the same level of importance or impact.

Some decisions have greater consequences or contribute more significantly to the overall objective or outcome. Therefore, weighting decision points helps to assign relative importance or priority to different choices or actions.

By assigning weights, decision makers can allocate resources, time, and effort appropriately, focusing on the decisions that have a more substantial influence on achieving the desired goals.

This approach ensures that valuable resources are directed efficiently and that attention is given to critical decision points, optimizing the decision-making process.

Organizing decisions based on their weighting allows for a systematic and structured approach to problem-solving. Decision makers can categorize decisions into different tiers or levels based on their relative importance or impact.

High-weight decisions, which have significant consequences or long-term effects, can be given more attention, analysis, and consideration. Lower-weight decisions, on the other hand, may require less scrutiny or can be delegated to other team members or automated systems.

By organizing decisions in this manner, decision makers can prioritize their efforts, allocate resources effectively, and focus on the decisions that will have the greatest overall impact. This systematic approach enables efficient decision-making, streamlines the problem-solving process, and increases the likelihood of achieving desired outcomes.

13. Solving For the Lesser of Two Evils

In the realm of problem-solving, decision makers often find themselves confronted with situations where there are no ideal or favorable choices.

Instead, they are faced with a range of options, all of which carry negative consequences or undesirable outcomes. This predicament forces decision makers to engage in the delicate process of assessing and selecting the least bad option available to them.

The process of choosing between "all bad options" requires a nuanced approach and careful consideration of various factors. Decision makers must first recognize and accept the limitations of the available options.

It is crucial to acknowledge that sometimes circumstances dictate a lack of perfect solutions, leaving them with choices that may cause harm, inconvenience, or dissatisfaction in one way or another.

To navigate this challenging landscape, decision makers must adopt a systematic and analytical mindset. They need to objectively evaluate the potential risks, drawbacks, and benefits associated with each option.

This evaluation may involve considering short-term versus long-term consequences, weighing immediate impact against future implications, and assessing the varying degrees of harm or compromise involved.

Furthermore, decision makers must prioritize their objectives and values when selecting the least bad option. They need to identify which outcomes align more closely with their core principles and overarching goals. This process requires a deep understanding of the context, stakeholders involved, and the potential ripple effects that each option might trigger.

Ultimately, the act of choosing between all bad options demands a certain level of resilience, pragmatism, and ethical reasoning. Decision makers must acknowledge the inherent imperfections of the situation and make the best possible choice under the circumstances. While it may not be a perfect solution, selecting the least bad option demonstrates a commitment to mitigating harm and striving for the best possible outcome within the constraints of the situation.

By acknowledging the reality of choosing between all bad options and approaching the decision-making process with a thoughtful and systematic mindset, decision makers can navigate through challenging situations with a greater sense of clarity and purpose.

Although the options may not be ideal, the focus remains on minimizing harm and optimizing the outcome to the best extent possible.

In such instances, various classic staff reduction problems arise, presenting decision makers with the challenging task of evaluating unfavorable options. Staffing issues, in particular, encompass a range of problem domains where finding satisfactory solutions can be complex and intricate.

While the absence of ideal or favorable choices extends beyond staffing alone, personnel-related problems consistently introduce multifaceted and nuanced factors that demand careful consideration when devising effective solutions.

Cutting Staff or Going Out of Business

One of the most daunting staffing problems a company can face is the necessity to cut staff or face the possibility of going out of business entirely.

This situation often arises when a company is experiencing significant financial challenges or undergoing a strategic restructuring. When confronted with this dilemma, decision makers are tasked with making incredibly tough choices that can have profound implications for the organization and its employees.

Cutting staff as a means to salvage the business involves a delicate balancing act. On one hand, reducing the workforce can help reduce operational costs, enhance efficiency, and align the company's size with its current financial realities. On the other hand, such actions may lead to a loss of valuable talent, decreased employee morale, and a potential impact on the company's overall productivity and long-term viability.

In these circumstances, decision makers must approach staff reductions with sensitivity and strategic foresight. They need to consider factors such as the criticality of various roles, the potential for reassignment or retraining, and the impact on the remaining employees.

Open and transparent communication becomes vital, as it helps foster trust and understanding among the workforce. Additionally, providing support mechanisms such as outplacement services or assistance in finding new employment opportunities can mitigate the negative impact on affected employees and demonstrate a commitment to their well-being.

Ultimately, the decision to cut staff or face going out of business is a significant turning point for any organization. It demands careful analysis of the company's financial health, evaluation of alternative strategies, and a clear understanding of the potential consequences.

While staff reductions can be an extremely difficult and emotional process, approaching it with empathy, fairness, and a long-term perspective can help strike a delicate balance between preserving the business and minimizing the impact on its employees.

Arbitrary Across Department Staffing Cuts

When a company decides to implement a reduction in staff across departments by a fixed percentage, such as 20% each, it is important to recognize that the impact of this strategy may not be evenly distributed.

While the intention behind such an approach is to achieve fairness and consistency, the reality is that the consequences can vary significantly across different teams and departments. Smaller teams or departments often bear the brunt of across-the-board staff reductions.

With fewer members to begin with, the loss of even a single team member can result in a significant increase in workload for the remaining employees. This sudden surge in responsibilities can lead to feelings of overwhelm, stress, and fatigue, ultimately affecting morale and job satisfaction.

As a consequence, team members may experience a sense of resentment towards the company, potentially resulting in decreased productivity, increased absenteeism, and even a higher likelihood of turnover.

To mitigate the negative effects of across-the-board reductions, decision makers should adopt a more nuanced and tailored approach. Instead of solely relying on fixed percentage cuts, they can consider factors such as the workload distribution, the criticality of specific roles or departments, and the potential for reallocation or outsourcing of certain tasks.

By taking these considerations into account, decision makers can minimize the disproportionate impact on smaller teams, preserve team morale, and ensure that the workload remains manageable for the remaining employees.

Disproportionate Staffing Cuts

When faced with the need to make disproportionate cuts across departments, such as targeting middle management rather than lower-wage employees like those in manufacturing, decision makers must carefully navigate the complex dynamics of organizational restructuring.

In these situations, projecting confident leadership becomes crucial. While it may seem counterintuitive to cut middle management roles that provide oversight and guidance, it is essential to evaluate the organization's structure and identify areas where redundancies or inefficiencies exist.

Making these strategic adjustments allows decision makers to streamline operations and improve cost-effectiveness.

However, it is equally important to communicate these decisions transparently, emphasizing the organization's long-term goals, and instilling confidence in the remaining employees that the changes are aimed at preserving the company's viability and ensuring a sustainable future.

Hiring Freezes

The implementation of hiring freezes in organizations can have unintended consequences, as they introduce a series of adverse effects. While hiring freezes are often imposed to control costs or manage uncertain market conditions, they can inadvertently lead to several challenges.

For instance, open job requisitions intended to replace retired employees or address severe personnel shortages due to market conditions may remain unfilled.

This can result in increased workloads for existing employees, decreased productivity, and potential burnout. Moreover, customer service or sales response times may suffer, impacting the organization's ability to meet client demands and maintain customer satisfaction.

Arbitrary and across-the-board hiring freezes can have disastrous effects on an organization. While the intention behind such freezes may be to reduce costs, the unintended consequences can be detrimental. Decision makers should recognize the potential negative impact and seek a more strategic approach when curtailing hiring.

Rather than a complete stoppage, a more balanced strategy could involve prioritizing critical roles or departments and strategically filling positions that are essential to maintain operational efficiency and meet customer demands.

To mitigate the adverse effects of hiring freezes, decision makers need to empower organizations with a more strategic approach. This approach involves careful analysis of staffing needs, identifying positions critical for organizational success, and making informed decisions on where to allocate limited resources.

It is crucial to assess the potential risks and evaluate the long-term implications of leaving essential roles unfilled. In addition, organizations can focus on alternative strategies such as upskilling or reskilling existing employees to address talent shortages and enhance workforce flexibility.

Through a thoughtful and strategic approach to hiring freezes, decision makers can effectively minimize the negative impact on the organization, while simultaneously maintaining employee morale and ensuring the adequate support of essential functions despite the imposed restrictions.

Cut One $100K Job or Two $50K Jobs?

When faced with the dilemma of whether to cut a higher paid employee or two employees at lower wages, decision managers are confronted with a challenging trade-off. Urgent priorities and the need for staffing reductions can often create difficult choices.

Cutting a higher paid $100K job may provide immediate cost savings but can also have broader implications on employee morale. Losing a single individual who holds a higher position and earns a larger salary may lead to a sense of shock, anxiety, and reduced morale among the remaining workforce.

Conversely, cutting two $50K jobs might distribute the impact more evenly but can result in a broader reduction of skill sets and a potential decline in team morale due to the loss of multiple colleagues.

Balancing the financial considerations with the potential morale and productivity impacts requires careful evaluation of the specific circumstances, the roles involved, and the overall organizational objectives.

In this situation, decision managers need to consider the larger picture and carefully assess the trade-offs. They should evaluate the immediate cost savings, the criticality of each role, and the potential impact on team dynamics and morale.

Open and transparent communication is crucial during such times, as it helps address concerns, provide clarity on the decision-making process, and demonstrate a commitment to the well-being of the remaining employees.

Additionally, managers can explore alternative measures, such as reallocating responsibilities or restructuring teams, to minimize the negative impact on morale while achieving the necessary staffing reductions.

By taking a thoughtful and empathetic approach to this dilemma, decision managers can strike a balance between financial considerations and maintaining a positive and motivated workforce.

Making Shift Changes

Implementing a shift change to multiple shift environments can have significant implications for staff turnover. While such changes may be necessary to accommodate increased workload or optimize operational efficiency, they can disrupt the established routines and work-life balance of employees.

Shifting from a traditional single-shift model to a multi-shift system introduces new scheduling complexities, potential fatigue concerns, and challenges in maintaining effective communication and coordination across different shifts.

These changes can lead to increased stress and dissatisfaction among employees, particularly if the shifts are irregular or interfere with personal commitments.

Mitigating the negative effects of this transition and minimizing staff turnover requires decision makers to involve employees in the decision-making process, provide adequate training and support to adapt to the new shift patterns, and establish mechanisms for ongoing feedback and communication to address any concerns or issues that arise.

These steps are crucial in ensuring a smoother transition and maintaining a satisfied and productive workforce. Taking into account the well-being and needs of the employees during this transition is essential for decision makers who aim to maintain a motivated and engaged workforce while optimizing operational efficiency.

Forcing Staffing Reductions Through Policy Changes

In certain situations, organizations may seek to achieve staffing reductions by implementing policy changes aimed at encouraging attrition.

One approach is to introduce new policies that require employees to spend a mandatory amount of time in the office, especially in a post-pandemic world where remote work has become prevalent.

By establishing such policies, decision makers hope to create a subtle incentive for employees who prefer remote work to consider voluntary departures.

This strategy aims to reduce staff numbers without the need for direct layoffs or terminations, thereby minimizing the associated costs and potential negative impacts on employee morale and company culture.

Implementing early retirement incentives is another policy change that organizations may employ to achieve staffing reductions. By offering attractive packages or benefits to eligible employees who are nearing retirement age, decision makers can create a voluntary departure opportunity.

This approach allows employees who are ready for retirement to depart willingly, opening up positions that can be strategically left unfilled or restructured to optimize operational efficiency.

Early retirement incentives provide a more positive and potentially more attractive option for staff reduction compared to mandatory layoffs, as they empower employees to make their own decisions about their future while enabling organizations to achieve their staffing goals.

By utilizing policy changes and incentives to encourage attrition and voluntary departures, organizations can navigate staffing reductions with a more humane approach.

This strategy not only minimizes the disruption and potential negative effects of mandatory layoffs but also provides employees with choices and flexibility regarding their career paths.

It is crucial for decision makers to design these policies and incentives thoughtfully, ensuring clear communication, fairness, and transparency throughout the process. By doing so, organizations can effectively manage their workforce while maintaining positive employee relations and fostering a culture of respect and support.

People vs. Artificial Intelligence

The advent of artificial intelligence (AI) presents a significant challenge in the realm of staffing. AI has the potential to revolutionize various aspects of business operations and can offer substantial benefits to companies.

By leveraging AI technologies, organizations can streamline processes, improve efficiency, and reduce the long-term need for extensive staffing in certain areas.

For instance, AI-powered systems can enhance customer service by providing quick response times and personalized information tailored to individual consumers.

They can also automate repetitive and mundane tasks, freeing up human resources to focus on more complex and strategic endeavors. The implementation of AI has the potential to significantly optimize workforce allocation and drive financial gains for businesses.

However, the potential reduction in staffing that AI brings forth poses a dilemma for decision makers. While there are clear advantages in terms of efficiency and cost savings, the introduction of AI technologies raises concerns about the impact on the existing workforce.

Decision makers must grapple with the ethical and moral considerations of replacing human employees with AI systems, which can lead to job displacement and unemployment.

Furthermore, the introduction of AI may require reskilling or upskilling of the remaining workforce to adapt to new roles and responsibilities, creating additional challenges.

Striking the right balance between leveraging AI technologies for increased efficiency and preserving the well-being and livelihoods of employees is a complex decision that requires careful thought and consideration.

As organizations explore the potential of AI to reduce staffing, decision makers must navigate the dilemma it poses. They must weigh the benefits of improved efficiency, cost savings, and enhanced customer experiences against the ethical implications and potential impact on the workforce.

In embracing AI technologies, companies should also consider implementing proactive measures to support and retrain employees whose roles may be affected.

By taking a responsible and empathetic approach, decision makers can strive for a balance between harnessing the benefits of AI and ensuring the welfare and livelihoods of their employees in the face of technological advancements.

Closing Offices or Retail Locations

In the course of business evolution, companies often find themselves in a position where they need to make difficult choices regarding reducing or consolidating office or retail locations.

These decisions can significantly impact staffing and require careful consideration from decision makers. Determining which business locations to close involves a complex problem-solving process influenced by various internal and external factors.

Decision makers must weigh several factors when considering office or retail closures. These include financial considerations such as operational costs, lease agreements, and market demand for the company's products or services in specific locations.

Additionally, the geographic distribution of customers and competition, changing demographic trends, and shifts in consumer behavior play crucial roles in shaping these decisions.

External factors, such as economic conditions, regulatory changes, or unexpected events like a pandemic, can also influence the need for office or retail closures.

Furthermore, decision makers need to assess the impact of closures on employees, considering potential job losses, the feasibility of reassignment, and the overall impact on staff morale and productivity.

Ultimately, choosing which business locations to close is a complex balancing act that demands a thorough analysis of both internal and external factors. Decision makers must carefully evaluate financial implications, market conditions, and the impact on employees.

By incorporating data-driven analysis, proactive planning, and a thoughtful approach to employee well-being, businesses can navigate the process of closing offices or retail locations more effectively, striving to achieve the optimal outcome while considering the broader dynamics of the industry and market conditions.

Businesses can navigate the process of closing offices or retail locations more effectively, striving to achieve the optimal outcome while considering the broader dynamics of the industry and market conditions, by incorporating data-driven analysis, proactive planning, and a thoughtful approach to employee well-being.

Navigating Staffing Challenges in Response to Business Environment Changes

Businesses often face significant changes in their business environment, such as product obsolescence or shifts in industry trends.

When confronted with such circumstances, it becomes crucial for businesses to adapt and evolve, or else face the risk of failure. These transformative changes often force organizations to reassess their strategies, make critical decisions, and, in some cases, restructure their staffing.

One notable trend in response to changes in the nature of goods or services sold is the outsourcing of certain functions. For example, in the 1980s, the outsourcing of software development emerged as a way for companies to leverage specialized expertise and reduce costs.

This shift allowed organizations to focus on their core competencies while relying on external software development firms to handle specific tasks.

Similarly, the outsourcing of manufacturing to international locations with cheaper labor costs has been a prevalent practice. This strategy enables businesses to remain competitive by capitalizing on cost advantages, leveraging global supply chains, and accessing specialized manufacturing capabilities.

However, these outsourcing decisions have significant implications for staffing, as they may involve workforce reductions in certain areas while requiring new skill sets or workforce expansions in others.

When businesses encounter changes in the nature of their goods or services sold, decision makers must carefully assess the evolving landscape and make strategic choices that align with their organizational goals. Adapting to industry or technological shifts may require reskilling or upskilling the existing workforce to meet new demands.

Additionally, it may involve hiring external expertise, forming strategic partnerships, or considering outsourcing options to ensure optimal utilization of resources and cost efficiencies.

Throughout these processes, open and transparent communication with employees is essential, helping them understand the reasons behind the changes and providing support mechanisms to navigate potential transitions.

By embracing change, businesses can seize opportunities, maintain relevance in evolving markets, and strategically manage staffing to align with new business realities.

Example: The Netflix Effect

The rise of Netflix and its transformative impact on the home video rental industry exemplifies the "Netflix Effect." By introducing a subscription-based DVD rental-by-mail service and later transitioning to a digital streaming platform, Netflix revolutionized how people consume movies and TV shows.

This technological disruption had far-reaching consequences, including a significant impact on staffing within the industry. As the popularity of Netflix soared, traditional video rental giants like Blockbuster Video struggled to adapt to this new paradigm.

The shift from physical rental stores to rental-by-mail and later online streaming necessitated a substantial reassessment of staffing needs and operational strategies. Blockbuster, being slow to recognize and embrace the changing landscape, faced immense challenges and ultimately succumbed to the pressure, filing for bankruptcy in 2010.

The Netflix Effect serves as a powerful case study highlighting the critical importance of adapting to technological disruptions and the subsequent implications for staffing in an evolving industry. It also shows how Netflix was able to recognize a similar risk and transition to a purely streaming-based delivery environment.

14. Expediency

Expediency, the desire to achieve quick results, can be both a blessing and a curse in problem-solving endeavors. While there are situations where speed is crucial, acting hastily without proper direction can often lead to subpar outcomes that fail to meet the needs of both the business sponsor and the project team.

The pressure to deliver quickly may cause corners to be cut, important steps to be overlooked, and essential considerations to be neglected. As a result, the rushed results not only waste precious financial resources but also squander the efforts and capabilities of the project team.

When individuals are compelled to work under such constraints of expediency, it can have demoralizing effects. The constant demand for quick turnarounds without sufficient guidance or resources places undue stress on the team members, eroding their confidence and job satisfaction.

The focus on speed over quality can diminish the sense of pride in their work and their ability to deliver their best. Over time, this can lead to decreased motivation, increased turnover, and a decline in overall team morale, further exacerbating the challenges faced during problem-solving endeavors.

Cost vs. Money

Within the realm of problem-solving, one of the most prevalent and persistent dilemmas is the perpetual struggle between the available funds and the actual cost of achieving a desired deliverable.

This conundrum often arises when business sponsors have clear objectives and expectations, but the allocated budget falls short of the necessary resources to fulfill those ambitions.

It sets the stage for a delicate balancing act, where the desire for a high-quality solution collides with the financial constraints at hand.

Under such circumstances, the process of downscaling becomes a frequent recourse. Downscaling involves adjusting the scope, scale, or features of a project to align with the available resources.

While it can be an effective strategy to ensure completion within budgetary limitations, it often results in compromised outcomes.

The final product may be an immature version that fails to fully meet the initial objectives or a stalled deliverable waiting for additional funding to reach its intended potential.

This dynamic highlights the perennial struggle between the ideal solution and the practical constraints imposed by financial realities.

Too Much Detail

In the realm of problem-solving and project implementation, an excessive focus on detail can become a stumbling block, hindering progress and delaying the actual start of a project.

Overanalyzing requirements, involving an abundance of stakeholders, conducting endless planning sessions, and over-designing the deliverable can all contribute to a state of analysis paralysis.

This state is driven by a fear of failure and a desire to cover every possible angle, resulting in a significant portion of the project's timeline being consumed by upfront efforts.

When roughly 80% of the project becomes occupied with these detailed activities, it becomes evident that the scale has tipped too far. The excess of bureaucratic procedures and intricate planning can stifle the momentum needed to move forward with actual implementation.

The longer the project remains in this phase, the greater the risk of missed opportunities, changing circumstances, and diminishing returns. To break free from this pattern, it becomes crucial to cut through the bureaucracy and push the project forward, recognizing that the pursuit of perfection in every detail can impede progress and hinder timely and effective solutions.

Finding the right balance between planning and execution is essential. While initial groundwork and careful consideration are vital, it's equally important to maintain a sense of pragmatism and agility.

Streamlining processes, prioritizing key requirements, and empowering decision-makers to make informed choices can help circumvent the trap of excessive detail.

By taking calculated risks and fostering a culture that values action, projects can move beyond the paralysis of analysis and start making tangible progress toward achieving their objectives.

Minimum Viable Product vs. Over-design

In the context of startups with limited funding, the pressure to create a product that can generate sales and attract additional funding can be immense. This often leads to the concept of a 'minimum viable product' (MVP) being introduced.

An MVP encompasses the essential features and functionality required for the product to be viable in the market, while also providing hints or a roadmap for future iterations and enhancements.

When core functionality drives decision-making, a well-executed MVP can pave the way for success. However, if the MVP is solely constrained by budget or time, the results are often mediocre at best, failing to meet customer expectations or deliver a compelling value proposition.

On the opposite end of the spectrum are products that lean towards over-design, incorporating unnecessary bells and whistles that could be expanded upon in future iterations.

While such designs may appear glorious and impressive on the surface, they often suffer from a critical drawback: they lack tangible outcomes when the funding inevitably runs out.

The resources invested in extensive and elaborate designs could have been better allocated to core functionality or essential features that could have made a more immediate impact. Over-designing can lead to a grand vision but little substance, leaving stakeholders and potential customers dissatisfied and questioning the practical value of the product.

Striking the right balance between an MVP and over-design is a delicate task. It requires a clear understanding of the core needs and value proposition of the product, as well as careful consideration of resource limitations.

By focusing on delivering a minimum viable product that fulfills the key requirements and provides a solid foundation for future growth, startups can maximize their chances of success.

This approach allows for the validation of key assumptions, gathering valuable customer feedback, and iterating based on real-world experiences, all while staying mindful of budgetary constraints and the need for timely progress.

Overworking a Problem

In the realms of engineering and scientific pursuits, there exists a common tendency to overwork a problem. This habit often manifests in the form of continuously refining a solution beyond any recognizable need or adding features to a product that will be utilized by less than 1% of its customers.

While the pursuit of perfection can be admirable, it can also be detrimental when it hinders progress and fails to yield substantial benefits. In these cases, the adage 'perfection is the enemy of the good' rings true.

In certain domains, iterating over a problem solution may be essential for achieving optimal outcomes. However, in other contexts, overworking a problem can result in unnecessary costs, delays, and minimal benefits. The quest for perfection can drain valuable resources, both in terms of time and finances, without proportionate returns.

Instead of delivering an adequate solution within a reasonable timeframe, the relentless pursuit of perfection can lead to diminishing returns and missed opportunities.

Recognizing the fine line between refining a solution and overworking a problem is crucial. It requires a clear understanding of the problem domain, the needs and expectations of the stakeholders, and the cost-benefit analysis of further iterations.

It is important to strike a balance between investing effort in refining the solution to a satisfactory level and recognizing when additional work is yielding diminishing returns.

By prioritizing the delivery of a solution that meets the essential requirements and offers tangible benefits, engineers and scientists can steer clear of needless expenses and delays while maximizing the value they provide.

Keeping the focus on what truly matters and avoiding overworking a problem enables professionals to streamline their efforts and achieve meaningful results efficiently.

Solutions That Are "Close Enough For All Practical Purposes"

In problem-solving, there are situations where a problem lends itself to a wide range of potential solutions. Additionally, there are instances where the solution delivered may already be 90% aligned with the desired goals.

However, the insatiable desire for perfection can often trap individuals in a vicious circle of endless iterations, constantly seeking a solution that is marginally better. This tendency to continuously strive for a flawless outcome can hinder progress and waste valuable time and resources.

It is important to recognize that not all problems require an ideal or perfect solution. In many cases, a solution that is 'just fine' or 'close enough' can adequately meet the needs and goals at hand. These solutions may not be flawless, but they are functionally effective and provide a reasonable level of value.

It becomes imperative to resist the urge to iterate endlessly over multiple 'acceptable options' in search of an incremental improvement that may not significantly impact the end result.

By embracing the concept of 'good enough' solutions, individuals can free themselves from the cycle of perpetual refinement and focus their efforts on other critical aspects of problem-solving.

This approach allows for quicker implementation, more efficient resource utilization, and a greater ability to address additional challenges or opportunities.

Recognizing when a solution is 'close enough for all practical purposes' empowers problem-solvers to make informed decisions and allocate their time and energy wisely.

Solutions Searching For a Problem

In the realm of innovation and product development, it is not uncommon for organizations to conceive solutions that appear to offer significant benefits and potential market acceptance.

However, upon closer examination, these solutions often find themselves in a puzzling predicament—they are searching for a problem to solve.

Despite their perceived advantages, these offerings struggle to find a compelling and well-defined problem or need in the market that they can effectively address.

Organizations facing the challenge of solutions searching for a problem may encounter difficulties in gaining traction and achieving widespread adoption. Without a clear problem to solve, the value proposition of these solutions remains elusive, making it challenging to resonate with target customers or garner significant market interest.

In such cases, it becomes crucial for organizations to revisit their understanding of customer needs, conduct thorough market research, and refine their product or service to align it with a genuine problem or demand.

By redirecting their efforts towards addressing real-world challenges, organizations can increase their chances of success and better position themselves in the competitive landscape.

Evaluating Consequences

Expediency holds significant importance in problem-solving and product development, especially when considering time-to-market factors.

However, it is crucial to evaluate the consequences of expediency and understand the potential impacts that arise from rushing a solution to meet an artificial timeframe.

While speed can offer advantages in competitive markets, hasty decision-making and shortcuts can have long-lasting repercussions.

One consequence of missing the window of opportunity due to a lack of expediency is the potential loss of market share and competitive advantage.

In fast-paced industries, being late to market can mean missed opportunities to capture customers, secure partnerships, or establish a strong foothold. This delay can allow competitors to gain a head start, eroding the potential success of the solution.

Additionally, rushing a solution to meet an artificial timeframe can result in compromised quality, performance, or functionality. This can lead to customer dissatisfaction, negative reviews, and a tarnished reputation, ultimately hindering long-term success.

Moreover, the impacts of rushing a solution can extend to the internal aspects of an organization. The pressure to deliver within a constrained timeframe may place excessive strain on the development team, potentially leading to burnout, decreased morale, and compromised work quality.

Rushed solutions may also require additional resources, including costly fixes or rework, which can strain budgets and hinder future innovation efforts.

It is essential to carefully weigh the consequences of expediency against the potential benefits, ensuring that the pursuit of speed does not sacrifice the quality, viability, and sustainability of the solution.

Failing to meet customer expectations due to a premature product launch can have detrimental consequences for a business. When a product is rushed to market without undergoing thorough testing or refinement, it can result in subpar quality, functionality issues, or missing features that customers anticipated.

This can lead to customer dissatisfaction, negative reviews, and even reputational damage, ultimately impacting customer trust, brand loyalty, and future sales. Taking the time to ensure that a product is truly ready for launch, meeting or exceeding customer expectations, is essential for long-term success in the market.

15. Dealing With Influence and Listening to Money

In the dynamic landscape of problem-solving, decision-making, and leadership, there exists a curious phenomenon: the disproportionate influence wielded by individuals who may not possess the depth of knowledge, insight, or expertise that their positions suggest.

Throughout various spheres, be it in the development of a new product, the execution of a project, or even the overall direction of a company, the power of influence can often overshadow the merits of informed decision-making.

In this chapter, we explore the intriguing interplay between influence and expertise, delving into the challenges that arise when the voice of authority and decision-making rests in the hands of those who may not possess the requisite understanding or vision.

While influence can arise from various sources, including seniority, charisma, or financial clout, it is crucial to recognize that it is not always synonymous with competence.

The repercussions of relying solely on influential figures can be far-reaching, leading to missed opportunities, flawed strategies, and a lack of progress.

It is essential to understand that this discussion is not meant to undermine the value of influential individuals or dismiss their potential contributions.

Rather, it aims to highlight the importance of balancing influence with expertise, ensuring that decisions are grounded in a comprehensive understanding of the subject matter at hand.

By acknowledging the potential pitfalls of an undue reliance on influence, we can adopt a more holistic approach to problem-solving, one that combines the power of insight and the strength of authority to drive meaningful outcomes.

In the following sections, we will examine real-world scenarios where influence has overshadowed expertise, leading to suboptimal outcomes.

We will explore strategies for navigating these challenges and fostering a culture that encourages the integration of diverse perspectives, informed decision-making, and a willingness to listen to voices beyond the confines of influence alone.

"The Smartest People Work Somewhere Else"

Within the realm of management, a peculiar perception often takes hold: the belief that internal resources or expertise are inherently less valuable than what can be found elsewhere.

This mindset stems from various factors, such as the absence of up-to-date knowledge among senior staff or an overabundance of junior positions within a particular project area.

Consequently, organizations may inadvertently overlook the talents and insights of their own employees, assuming that external sources hold the key to innovation and problem-solving. However, this perspective fails to recognize the untapped potential that lies within the internal workforce and the unique advantages it brings to the table.

One contributing factor to the notion that the smartest people work somewhere else is the perception of a knowledge gap among senior staff. As industries rapidly evolve and new technologies emerge, it is not uncommon for long-standing executives and decision-makers to lack direct experience with the latest advancements.

This can lead to a sense of insecurity and a belief that external consultants or experts possess a superior understanding of the industry's current landscape.

However, it is crucial to remember that senior staff members bring invaluable institutional knowledge, historical context, and a deep understanding of the organization's culture and values.

By bridging the gap between their wisdom and the fresh perspectives of external talent, a powerful synergy can be created, fueling innovation and effective problem-solving.

Another factor that perpetuates the perception of greater value elsewhere is the prevalence of junior positions within a project area. When a team consists primarily of less experienced members, there may be a tendency to believe that external experts are necessary to fill the gaps in knowledge and skill.

While external expertise can certainly provide valuable insights and new perspectives, underestimating the potential of internal team members can be a missed opportunity.

Junior employees often possess a unique eagerness to learn, adapt quickly to new technologies, and bring fresh ideas to the table. By fostering an environment that empowers these individuals and provides them with the necessary guidance and mentorship, organizations can tap into a wellspring of untapped potential that rivals the expertise found elsewhere.

Use of Consultants

When decision-makers are presented with a choice, they often opt to engage outside consultants and organizations to develop strategy, design concepts, and lead project efforts.

This inclination can arise from various factors, including a lack of confidence in their own decision-making abilities or the desire to have an external scapegoat in case of failures.

While there are valid reasons for seeking external expertise, such as introducing new processes or addressing resource limitations, it is equally important to recognize the potential pitfalls of relying too heavily on consultants as a crutch.

One factor driving the use of consultants is the lack of confidence that some management teams may have in their own decision-making abilities. When faced with complex challenges or unfamiliar territories, decision-makers may feel more comfortable relying on external consultants who bring specialized knowledge and a fresh perspective.

This allows them to shift the responsibility of decision-making and potential risks to an external entity. However, it is crucial to strike a balance between leveraging external expertise and nurturing internal capabilities, as over-reliance on consultants can stifle the growth and development of internal talent.

Another circumstance where the use of outside consultants becomes advantageous is when introducing new processes that encounter resistance from staff members reluctant to change.

External consultants can provide an objective viewpoint, independent from existing company dynamics, and help facilitate the adoption of new practices.

Their expertise and experience in managing change can mitigate internal resistance and foster a smoother transition. However, organizations should also prioritize internal change management efforts to empower and engage employees, ensuring their voices are heard and their concerns addressed throughout the process.

The size of an effort and projected long-term staffing needs can also lead decision-makers to turn to external consultants. When an organization lacks the necessary resources or expertise to execute a large-scale project, consultants can provide the required capabilities and augment the existing team.

This temporary injection of external talent can bring fresh ideas, specialized skills, and experience with similar projects.

However, it is crucial to view the engagement with consultants as a strategic partnership rather than a complete dependency, with a focus on knowledge transfer and building internal capacity for future initiatives.

While there are valid reasons for engaging outside consultants, it is essential to be mindful of the potential drawbacks. Overreliance on consultants can create a culture of dependency, where internal decision-making capabilities and problem-solving skills stagnate.

It can also result in a lack of ownership and accountability within the organization, as blame can be shifted to external parties if something goes wrong.

Organizations must strike a balance between leveraging external expertise when needed and investing in the development of internal talent and decision-making capabilities.

Relying on Third Parties That Don't Really Understand Your Business

One common pitfall in decision-making occurs when organizations place their trust in external parties that possess general industry knowledge but lack a deep understanding of their specific business.

This reliance on third parties can lead to solutions that, while seemingly reasonable on the surface, fail to fully meet the unique needs and objectives of the organization.

These external entities may emphasize elements of a solution that provide little benefit to the business or its client base, as they lack the contextual understanding necessary to identify the true priorities and weigh the importance of various objectives and criteria.

An expert in a given field may possess a strong understanding of business principles and practices, but that does not guarantee a comprehensive understanding of the intricacies and unique dynamics of your specific business.

Specialized knowledge of your organization's industry and context is essential to truly grasp the nuances, objectives, and challenges that shape your business's decision-making processes.

When decision-makers engage with third parties unfamiliar with the intricacies of their business, there is a risk of solutions being skewed towards generic industry practices or trends rather than tailored to the specific challenges and opportunities faced by the organization.

While external perspectives can provide valuable insights and fresh ideas, it is crucial to ensure that these insights are applied within the context of the business's unique requirements. Failure to account for this distinction can result in misaligned strategies, wasted resources, and missed opportunities for innovation and growth.

The lack of in-depth understanding exhibited by external parties can manifest in their inability to grasp the weighting of objectives and criteria that are crucial for the organization.

They may place undue emphasis on elements of a solution that, upon closer examination, do not align with the organization's priorities or contribute significantly to its success.

This mismatch between the perceived importance of certain aspects and the actual needs of the business can lead to suboptimal decision-making and hinder progress towards achieving the organization's strategic goals.

Furthermore, external parties who lack a deep understanding of the business may overlook or underestimate the unique nuances of the organization's client base.

They may fail to recognize the specific needs, preferences, and behaviors of the target audience, resulting in solutions that do not resonate with customers or adequately address their pain points. This can lead to missed opportunities for customer satisfaction, loyalty, and ultimately, business growth.

To mitigate the risks associated with relying on third parties that don't fully understand the business, decision makers should prioritize the inclusion of internal stakeholders who possess intimate knowledge of the business's intricacies.

It is crucial to engage in open and transparent communication with external parties, providing them with comprehensive insights into the organization's objectives, values, and customer base.

Collaborative partnerships that combine external expertise with internal knowledge can yield more holistic and effective solutions that align with the organization's unique requirements.

Don't Equate Money to Success – Some People Really Are Lucky

In the realm of business and success, it is important to recognize that the acquisition of wealth or rising to a position of power does not necessarily indicate a person's intelligence, business acumen, or leadership qualities.

While it is true that many individuals have achieved financial success through their endeavors, it is crucial to understand that luck and fortunate circumstances can play a significant role in their achievements.

Simply being in the right place at the right time can propel someone to great financial heights, even without possessing exceptional skills or leadership capabilities.

It is a common fallacy to equate financial success with inherent wisdom or expertise in the business world. While some individuals may have amassed significant wealth, it does not guarantee that they possess the necessary qualities to lead and foster future success.

Making millions of dollars or attaining a high-ranking position within an organization does not automatically translate to effective leadership or the ability to empower others.

True success should be measured by a holistic evaluation of a person's skills, character, and impact, rather than solely focusing on monetary achievements.

In reality, luck can significantly influence an individual's trajectory, presenting them with opportunities that others may not have had.

Chance encounters, fortuitous market conditions, or being in the right place at the right time can contribute to a person's financial success without necessarily reflecting their business acumen or leadership qualities.

It is important to recognize that luck plays a role in various aspects of life, including professional achievements, and that attributing success solely to personal attributes can be misleading.

To truly assess a person's capabilities and potential for long-term success, it is crucial to delve beyond monetary achievements and consider their leadership qualities, vision, adaptability, and ability to inspire and empower others.

Effective leadership goes beyond financial gains and encompasses the ability to build sustainable businesses, nurture talent, create positive organizational cultures, and make meaningful contributions to society.

By adopting a more holistic perspective, we can move beyond the allure of financial success and focus on cultivating well-rounded leaders who can drive lasting and impactful change.

By acknowledging the role of luck and reframing the notion of success beyond monetary achievements, we can cultivate a more nuanced understanding of what truly defines accomplishment in the business world.

In the subsequent sections, we will explore the qualities and attributes that contribute to effective leadership and delve into strategies for fostering a culture that values holistic success, empowering leaders, and making a positive difference in the lives of others.

Reputation Versus Results

In the realm of business, there exists a distinction between reputation and results. Many individuals can attain a significant level of reputation within a specific business, industry, or area of expertise.

These individuals may enjoy successful careers and be highly regarded for their accomplishments, often advancing the concepts of projects or products.

However, it is important to recognize that reputation does not always directly correlate with the ability to achieve tangible results, whether in terms of financial success or delivering on project deliverables. Past achievements do not guarantee future success, and an individual's capacity to deliver results can vary significantly.

One common pitfall is assuming that someone who achieved notable success in a previous role or venture will be equally successful in their subsequent opportunities.

For instance, a CEO who led a highly successful initial public offering (IPO) for their previous company may not necessarily be able to replicate the same level of results in their next endeavor.

The factors that contributed to their initial success may be specific to that particular context, and their skill set may be tailored to a narrow area of expertise. It is essential to evaluate individuals based on their ability to deliver results in diverse circumstances, rather than relying solely on their reputation or past achievements.

Reputation often stems from the recognition and praise garnered through accomplishments, but it is critical to distinguish between reputation-building activities and the ability to achieve concrete results.

While a strong reputation may open doors and create opportunities, it does not inherently guarantee success in every venture.

The capacity to consistently deliver results requires a combination of diverse skills, adaptability, problem-solving abilities, and a comprehensive understanding of the specific challenges and dynamics of each situation.

To mitigate the risk of placing undue emphasis on reputation without considering the ability to deliver results, it is important to adopt a more comprehensive evaluation framework.

This framework should encompass a holistic assessment of an individual's track record, their ability to adapt to new contexts, the breadth and depth of their expertise, and their capacity to navigate challenges and drive tangible outcomes.

Organizations can make more informed decisions by considering both reputation and results, thereby ensuring that individuals are not solely recognized for their past accomplishments but also evaluated based on their ability to achieve success in new and diverse environments.

Reputation and results are distinct aspects of professional achievement. While reputation can provide visibility and recognition, it should not be the sole determinant of an individual's capabilities.

By recognizing the nuances between reputation and the ability to deliver results, organizations can make more informed decisions and foster a culture that values both tangible outcomes and the qualities that contribute to sustained success.

The Celebrity Factor

The promotion of a product or service by a celebrity spokesman has been observed to be effective due to several reasons.

Firstly, celebrities often possess a large and dedicated fan base, creating a sense of familiarity and trust among their followers. This connection can influence consumer behavior, as individuals are more inclined to engage with a product or service endorsed by a beloved figure.

Additionally, celebrities are seen as trendsetters and influencers in popular culture, leading to a perception that their choices and preferences reflect the zeitgeist. As a result, their endorsement of a particular brand can create a sense of desirability and aspiration among consumers.

However, it is important to approach celebrity endorsements with a critical mindset. While celebrities may excel in their respective fields, their expertise or credibility on other topics can be questionable.

It is crucial to separate their influence in the realm of entertainment or sports from their ability to provide informed opinions on broader subjects.

In business environments, the overemphasis on the importance of celebrity can be misleading, as success in one area does not necessarily translate into expertise or wisdom in unrelated domains.

Whether it is a celebrity, a highly regarded industry expert, or a prestigious award winner, it is essential to evaluate their opinions and insights based on their merit and relevance to the specific context rather than granting unwarranted weight solely due to their fame or accolades.

16. Resolving The Least Common Denominator

In the world of problem-solving, it is essential to be resourceful and creative, seeking solutions that not only tackle specific issues but also possess the versatility to address multiple problems at once.

This approach not only saves time and effort but can lead to more comprehensive and sustainable resolutions.

Imagine a scenario where a business is facing several challenges simultaneously: declining sales, a lack of employee motivation, and rising operational costs.

While it might be tempting to devise separate strategies for each problem, a more astute approach would be to search for a single solution that can positively impact all three areas.

One exemplary path that demonstrates the power of a multi-purpose solution is "Employee Empowerment." By focusing on empowering employees, businesses can potentially tackle multiple issues:

> **Increasing Sales**: Empowered employees, who are given more autonomy and decision-making power, can better engage with customers, understand their needs, and provide personalized solutions, ultimately leading to improved sales figures.
>
> **Boosting Employee Motivation**: Granting employees more control over their work and involving them in decision-making processes can significantly enhance their motivation and job satisfaction. This increased enthusiasm and commitment can lead to a more productive and harmonious work environment.
>
> **Reducing Operational Costs**: Empowering employees often involves encouraging innovation and efficiency. Employees who feel valued and empowered are more likely to suggest process improvements and cost-saving measures, thus positively impacting the company's bottom line.

By identifying the common denominator among multiple challenges and devising a solution that addresses them simultaneously, problem solvers can unlock a host of benefits. Not only does this approach streamline the problem-solving process, but it also fosters a more cohesive and connected approach to tackling complex issues.

However, it is important to acknowledge that not all problems can be resolved through a single multi-purpose solution. Some issues may require specialized attention.

As problem solvers, it is essential to discern when a targeted approach is needed and when a multi-faceted solution can be applied for optimal results.

Additional Examples

Indeed, seeking out common elements and connections between different challenges can pave the way for innovative strategies that lead to more comprehensive and impactful resolutions.

When problem solvers take a holistic approach to understanding the underlying causes and relationships between various problems, they can create solutions that address the root issues rather than just the surface symptoms. Let's explore this concept further:

In problem-solving, it's easy to get caught up in treating each challenge as an isolated incident, but this approach may lead to short-term fixes that don't address the bigger picture.

By actively seeking out common elements and connections between different problems, we can:

1. **Uncover Root Causes**: Often, different problems may share underlying root causes. These root causes might not be immediately obvious, but by examining patterns and relationships, we can identify them. Solving these root causes can eliminate multiple problems at once, saving time and effort in the long run.

2. **Identify Overlapping Solutions**: Certain solutions might be applicable to multiple challenges. By recognizing these overlaps, we can implement one strategy that has a positive ripple effect on various aspects of the problem landscape.

3. **Leverage Synergy**: When multiple problems are interrelated, solving one problem can create a positive impact on others. The synergy generated by interconnected solutions can lead to more significant overall improvements.

4. **Avoid Unintended Consequences**: Addressing individual problems without considering their connections may lead to unintended consequences in other areas. Taking a comprehensive view helps avoid such pitfalls.

5. **Optimize Resource Utilization**: A multi-purpose solution that targets common elements can optimize the use of available resources. It minimizes duplication of efforts and maximizes the return on investment.

Let's consider an example to illustrate the power of seeking common elements and connections:

Example: Improving Community Health

A city is grappling with several health-related issues, such as a rise in chronic diseases, limited access to healthcare, and increasing healthcare costs. Instead of addressing each problem separately, a holistic approach could be taken:

Step 1: Conduct a comprehensive analysis of health data to identify common risk factors contributing to various chronic diseases.

Step 2: Develop a wellness program that promotes healthy living, targeting those common risk factors. This program could include initiatives like providing access to nutritious food, promoting physical activity, and offering health education workshops.

Step 3: Implement the wellness program in community centers, schools, and workplaces, thus increasing accessibility to healthcare resources.

Step 4: Collaborate with healthcare providers to offer preventative care and regular health check-ups as part of the program.

In this example, the holistic approach of addressing common risk factors not only improves community health but also reduces the burden on healthcare services and potentially lowers healthcare costs.

By encouraging problem solvers to think beyond individual issues and recognize the interconnected nature of problems, we can pave the way for transformative and sustainable solutions that have a more significant impact on society as a whole.

Example: Sustainable Urban Development

A growing city is facing several interconnected challenges related to urban development, environmental sustainability, and quality of life for its residents. Instead of tackling each problem in isolation, a holistic approach can be taken:

Challenge 1: Traffic Congestion

The city is experiencing severe traffic congestion during rush hours, leading to increased commute times and air pollution.

Challenge 2: Affordable Housing

With the city's population growth, there is a rising demand for affordable housing options for residents.

Challenge 3: Green Spaces

The city lacks sufficient green spaces and recreational areas, impacting the overall well-being of its residents.

Multi-Purpose Solution: Urban Green Corridors

The city can create urban green corridors that serve as a multi-purpose solution to address all three challenges simultaneously:

Step 1: Identify existing roads and transportation routes that are prone to heavy traffic congestion.

Step 2: Redesign these roads to include dedicated bus lanes, bike lanes, and pedestrian walkways.

Step 3: Plant trees and create green spaces alongside these corridors, providing shade, reducing air pollution, and beautifying the urban landscape.

Step 4: Implement zoning regulations that encourage mixed-use development along the corridors, including affordable housing options and commercial spaces.

Step 5: Connect the green corridors to existing parks and recreational areas, creating a network of green spaces throughout the city.

Benefits of Urban Green Corridors

There are several specific outcomes for the Urban Green Corridors:

Traffic Decongestion: By providing dedicated bus lanes and promoting alternative transportation methods, the urban green corridors can help alleviate traffic congestion, reducing commuting times and enhancing overall traffic flow.

Affordable Housing and Mixed-Use Development: The mixed-use development along the green corridors creates opportunities for affordable housing, making housing more accessible to residents while fostering vibrant and walkable neighborhoods.

Improved Air Quality and Urban Environment: The trees and green spaces planted along the corridors act as natural air filters, reducing air pollution and creating a healthier urban environment.

Enhanced Quality of Life: The presence of green spaces and recreational areas improves the overall well-being of residents by providing spaces for relaxation, exercise, and community interaction.

Sustainable Development: The focus on green infrastructure promotes sustainability and contributes to the city's efforts to mitigate the impacts of climate change.

In this example, the concept of urban green corridors offers a multi-purpose solution that tackles traffic congestion, affordable housing, and green space scarcity in an integrated and efficient manner.

By seeking common elements between these urban challenges, the city can implement a transformative strategy that brings positive changes to the lives of its residents while ensuring long-term sustainability.

17. How To Discover You're Wrong

Admitting and embracing the possibility of being wrong is a challenging but essential skill for personal and intellectual growth. This chapter focuses on cultivating humility, open-mindedness, and self-awareness to navigate the treacherous territory of uncertainty and ultimately arrive at better solutions.

It explores the psychological barriers that prevent individuals from acknowledging their mistakes or misconceptions and emphasizes the importance of recognizing these defense mechanisms in oneself.

By understanding the cognitive biases that influence our perceptions, readers are empowered to break free from the confines of preconceived notions and embrace a more objective and rational approach to problem-solving.

Throughout this chapter, practical techniques are discussed to help readers embrace the possibility of being wrong without feeling threatened or vulnerable.

One such approach involves actively seeking out diverse perspectives and constructive criticism, fostering an environment that encourages honest feedback and promotes intellectual humility.

Additionally, the chapter explores the significance of separating personal identity from ideas, allowing for a more detached and objective evaluation of one's own beliefs.

The Strength of One's Conviction Is No Measure of the Truth

The profound notion that the intensity of an individual's conviction does not necessarily reflect the accuracy or truthfulness of their beliefs. Throughout history, there have been countless examples that exemplify how deeply held convictions, while fervently defended, can often lead people astray from reality.

One such historical example is the belief in a flat Earth during the Age of Exploration. For centuries, many societies held the conviction that the

Earth was flat, and this belief was so ingrained that it became a widely accepted truth.

Sailors and explorers of that time navigated the seas with the unwavering conviction that by sailing westward, they would eventually reach the edge of the Earth and fall off.

However, as history unfolded, intrepid explorers like Christopher Columbus demonstrated the fallacy of this conviction by discovering new lands beyond the horizon, proving that the Earth was, indeed, round.

This example serves as a stark reminder that the strength of collective belief does not automatically validate the underlying truth of those beliefs. It illustrates the importance of subjecting our convictions to rigorous scrutiny and objective analysis.

Blindly adhering to strong convictions can hinder progress and impede the discovery of more accurate and effective solutions to problems.

Therefore, embracing intellectual humility and open-mindedness becomes paramount in the pursuit of uncovering the truth and achieving successful problem-solving outcomes.

By reflecting on historical instances like the flat Earth belief, readers are encouraged to question their own convictions and consider alternative viewpoints without prejudice.

Understanding that the strength of conviction alone is insufficient in determining truth allows individuals to adopt a more rational and evidence-based approach to problem-solving, fostering an environment where insights and knowledge can flourish unburdened by the constraints of dogma and unwarranted certainties.

In doing so, the journey towards discovering one's mistakes and arriving at better solutions becomes a more enlightened and fruitful endeavor.

Papillon: The Illusion of Flattery and Truth

"Papillon" - a term used to describe situations where individuals, often driven by a desire for approval and validation, seek feedback that is overwhelmingly positive.

This tendency to fish for compliments or reassuring responses is pervasive in various contexts, from personal appearance to creative work and problem-solving ideas.

The example of "How do I look?" perfectly encapsulates this behavior. People, like the Papillon and other prisoners, are often inclined to ask for opinions while secretly hoping for an affirmative response, such as "you look great."

While the intention may be harmless, the consequence is that truthful and constructive feedback becomes elusive. Friends and acquaintances, wanting to be supportive and avoid causing discomfort, may inadvertently provide insincere praise or withhold valuable criticism.

As readers contemplate this example, they are prompted to question the authenticity of the feedback they receive in their own lives. The chapter challenges individuals to consider whether they are truly getting the truth or merely hearing what others believe they want to hear.

This introspection highlights the importance of fostering a culture of honesty and constructive criticism in problem-solving scenarios.

To ascertain the truth, the chapter advocates for seeking feedback from a diverse range of sources, including those who may be less inclined to flattery and more willing to offer candid insights.

Constructive criticism, though often uncomfortable to receive, is a valuable asset in identifying weaknesses, blind spots, and opportunities for improvement.

Encouraging an environment where individuals can provide feedback without fear of repercussions enables more robust problem-solving processes and drives progress.

The concept of "Papillon" serves as a cautionary reminder that seeking validation at the expense of the truth can hinder personal and intellectual growth.

Repeating History: Changing Candidates, Unchanged Facts

In the context of political campaigns, where two candidates vie for the same office in different election cycles; while the candidates themselves may vary, the underlying question arises: Have the facts truly changed?

It is not uncommon in politics to witness candidates reemerge in subsequent elections, seeking the same office they once contested.

Despite the passage of time and potential changes in the political landscape, the core facts and challenges often remain constant. This recurrence presents a unique opportunity for reflection and analysis, as it prompts individuals to evaluate whether historical events and facts have genuinely evolved, or if they persist in a similar form.

Examining the repetition of candidates and campaigns, readers are encouraged to discern between genuine transformations and mere surface-level changes.

While the individuals may bring different perspectives and choices, fundamental issues and societal concerns might endure.

This raises questions about the effectiveness of previous problem-solving approaches and the need for fresh strategies to address persistent challenges.

By scrutinizing this pattern of history repeating itself, individuals can extract valuable lessons. It underscores the importance of understanding the root causes of problems and recognizing that merely replacing individuals or altering superficial aspects may not lead to substantive change.

A comprehensive and nuanced understanding of the facts is crucial to developing innovative and impactful solutions.

Furthermore, this examination of history repeating itself extends beyond the realm of politics. It serves as a reminder that, in various domains of life, we must critically evaluate whether the facts have indeed evolved before determining the most appropriate problem-solving approaches.

The chapter urges readers to engage in thorough research, data analysis, and collaboration to ensure that the solutions offered address the present realities rather than merely rehashing past actions.

Ultimately, confronting the notion of repeating history prompts individuals to adopt a forward-thinking and adaptable mindset. Instead of relying solely on past experiences, they learn to identify enduring truths, make informed decisions, and devise solutions that are truly tailored to the current context.

By embracing this approach, individuals can navigate the complexities of problem-solving with greater efficacy, ultimately leading to more positive and transformative outcomes.

As individuals delve deeper into the concept of "repeating history," they come to understand that historical patterns are not limited to the political sphere alone.

This recurring theme is evident across a spectrum of fields, from technology and business to social issues and personal relationships. Recognizing these patterns allows individuals to adopt a more proactive and insightful problem-solving approach that transcends the limitations of the past.

In technology and innovation, for instance, history often sees the emergence of revolutionary ideas or groundbreaking inventions that appear to be entirely novel.

However, upon closer examination, one can often trace the roots of these innovations back to earlier concepts that were not fully realized or implemented at the time. By acknowledging these historical antecedents, modern problem solvers can build upon existing knowledge, learn from past mistakes, and create more refined and effective solutions.

Similarly, in the realm of social issues, history often reveals deeply ingrained and systemic challenges that persist over time.

Racial discrimination, income inequality, and access to education are examples of societal problems that have a long history of recurrence.

By studying these patterns, individuals can gain a more profound understanding of the root causes, enabling them to develop comprehensive strategies that tackle the underlying issues, rather than merely addressing superficial symptoms.

On a personal level, recognizing patterns of behavior in relationships and decision-making can lead to greater self-awareness and growth.

People may find themselves repeatedly facing similar challenges or making the same mistakes, even across different contexts. By acknowledging these patterns, individuals can work towards breaking negative cycles and cultivating more positive and constructive habits.

While historical facts may serve as a foundation, problem solvers must approach each situation with fresh perspectives and adaptability. This forward-thinking mentality allows for innovative solutions that are both informed by the past and relevant to the present.

Fool Me Once, Shame on You: The Art of Learning from Mistakes

"Fool me once, shame on you; fool me twice, shame on me." This proverbial wisdom encapsulates a fundamental aspect of problem-solving and personal growth - the ability to learn from past mistakes and avoid repeating them.

The chapter delves into the idea that making mistakes is an inevitable part of the human experience. Everyone encounters errors, misjudgments, and failures at some point in their lives. While the initial mistake might be attributed to external factors or the actions of others, the real power lies in how one responds and processes the experience.

Fool me once: The first time a mistake or deception occurs, it serves as a crucial learning opportunity. It is natural to feel disappointed, betrayed, or hurt, but this initial experience should prompt individuals to reflect and analyze the situation.

Understanding what led to the mistake, what signs were missed, and what role personal choices played is essential for personal growth and future problem-solving.

Shame on you: When someone else deceives or takes advantage of an individual, the blame lies with the perpetrator. However, it is crucial not to absolve oneself entirely of responsibility. Accepting that a mistake was made and taking ownership of one's actions empowers individuals to make better choices in the future and avoid similar pitfalls.

Shame on me: If the same mistake occurs again, without taking corrective action or learning from the initial experience, the blame shifts to the individual.

Repeatedly falling into the same trap despite prior knowledge implies a failure to adapt, grow, or apply lessons learned. In such instances, the responsibility for the outcome lies with the person who did not take heed of past errors.

The chapter underscores the importance of embracing a growth mindset when confronted with mistakes or deception. Instead of dwelling on shame or blame, individuals should focus on learning from the experience, bolstering their problem-solving abilities, and developing resilience to navigate future challenges effectively.

By embracing the wisdom of "fool me once, shame on you; fool me twice, shame on me," readers are encouraged to cultivate self-awareness, make informed choices, and approach problem-solving with the humility to acknowledge and learn from their mistakes.

Armed with this mindset, individuals can forge a path of continuous improvement and make more informed, insightful decisions in all aspects of life.

18. How To Discover Someone Else Is Wrong

In our journey of problem-solving and seeking the truth, it's crucial to acknowledge the phenomenon of the "loudest voice in the room."

We have all experienced situations where an individual with a strong and dominant presence tends to dominate discussions, overshadowing quieter voices and drowning out differing perspectives.

Unfortunately, this prevailing attitude often leads to flawed conclusions and the overlooking of valuable insights.

The Loudest Voice

The *Illusion of Authority* often misleads us, as the volume of one's voice doesn't equate to the accuracy or validity of their statements.

The assumption that the loudest person is the most knowledgeable can be misleading. This impacts *Group Dynamics*, where dominant voices can influence decision-making processes in group settings, and a groupthink mentality can stifle constructive debate and inhibit better solutions.

It's essential to *Validate Information Over Volume*, focusing on the substance of arguments rather than the volume at which they are delivered, and encouraging evidence-based reasoning and objective analysis.

Embracing Diverse Perspectives is also key, creating an inclusive environment where everyone feels heard and valued, and encouraging diverse viewpoints to foster open dialogue and collaborative problem-solving.

The *Power of Active Listening* cannot be overstated. Actively engaging with others to understand their viewpoints, and identifying when the loudest voice may be dominating the discussion unfairly, is crucial. Also, *Humility and Admitting Mistakes* is important. Embrace humility, acknowledge that we can be wrong, be open to alternative ideas, and critically evaluate all perspectives.

In the quest for truth and effective problem-solving, we must be vigilant in recognizing the fallacy of equating volume with correctness.

Valuing diverse perspectives, actively listening, and promoting evidence-based reasoning enable us to overcome the allure of the loudest voice and collectively arrive at more informed and accurate conclusions.

Remember, the strength of our solutions lies not in the volume of our voices but in the depth of our understanding and the rigor of our critical thinking.

Asking The Right Question: To The Right People

In the pursuit of problem-solving and uncovering the truth, the art of asking questions plays a fundamental role. It's essential not just to ask any question but to ask the right question to the right people.

The *Power of Precision* is vital; a well-defined and precise question can lead to clearer answers and insights, while avoiding ambiguous or loaded questions prevents biased responses.

Identifying the Right People is also crucial. Determine who has the expertise or experience relevant to the issue and seek out diverse perspectives for a comprehensive understanding.

Tailoring Questions to Individuals involves customizing questions based on the knowledge and expertise of the person being asked. It's important to avoid overwhelming or oversimplifying questions, depending on the individual's background.

Recognizing Bias and Assumptions means being aware of your own biases while formulating questions and encouraging impartiality in responses by presenting questions free from preconceived notions.

Creating an Open and Safe Environment is about fostering a space where people feel comfortable sharing their thoughts and ideas, emphasizing that all input is valuable, regardless of seniority or status.

Empowering Cross-Functional Communication encourages collaboration between different departments or teams and facilitates information-sharing sessions to gather diverse insights.

Following Up and Clarifying requires actively listening to the responses received and seeking clarification when necessary, with additional questions to delve deeper into complex issues.

Adapting Your Approach involves staying flexible in questioning techniques based on the personalities and preferences of individuals and being prepared to modify inquiries as new information comes to light.

In conclusion, asking the right question to the right people is an art that significantly impacts problem-solving outcomes. By formulating precise questions, identifying relevant individuals, and fostering open communication, we can gather valuable insights and challenge assumptions effectively.

Remember, the process of discovery relies not only on the quality of our questions but also on our ability to listen and adapt our approach as we navigate the intricate landscape of seeking truth and finding solutions.

Determining the Motivations of Others (is envy involved)?

In the realm of problem-solving and seeking truth, we often encounter situations where influential figures, experts with decades of experience, or individuals with remarkable skills steer the conversation.

While their insights can be invaluable, it's essential to consider whether envy may play a role in the dynamics of the discussion. This exploration looks at how envy can manifest in such scenarios and how turning the tide of resentment can lead to more constructive problem-solving.

Recognizing the Impact of Influential Voices involves understanding that influencers and experienced individuals can sway discussions and shape opinions, and people may be hesitant to challenge or question the ideas put forth by those they admire or respect.

Envy and Resentment in the Face of Expertise can occur when individuals with less recognition or visibility feel overshadowed or undervalued, leading to envy as a response to perceived inequalities in attention or acknowledgment.

The *Role of Newcomers and Specific Skillsets* highlights how new individuals or those with unique expertise can disrupt established hierarchies, potentially evoking envy from those who have been more prominent in the field.

Navigating Envy for Constructive Discussions requires encouraging an open and inclusive environment where all perspectives are valued and addressing potential envy-related tensions by acknowledging individuals' contributions.

Promoting Collaboration and Learning emphasizes the importance of collaboration and teamwork in problem-solving, highlighting the value of diverse skillsets and how they can complement one another.

Fostering a Growth Mindset encourages individuals to view expertise and recognition as attainable through effort and learning, promoting the idea that everyone has unique contributions to offer.

Turning the Tide of Resentment involves facilitating discussions that embrace differences and encourage active participation, acknowledging and addressing any signs of envy and promoting open dialogue to understand its roots.

Celebrating Individual and Collective Achievements means recognizing and celebrating the achievements of both influential figures and newcomers, highlighting the importance of teamwork and collective progress.

The influence of prominent voices and experts can be both beneficial and challenging. However, it's crucial to consider the role of envy and resentment that may arise in such situations.

By fostering an inclusive environment that values diverse perspectives and promotes collaboration, we can turn the tide of resentment and create a space where all voices are heard and valued.

Embracing a growth mindset and celebrating individual and collective achievements contribute to a healthier problem-solving culture, allowing for more effective discovery and solutions.

Remember, the collective power of diverse voices outweighs the impact of envy, leading us to greater heights in our pursuit of truth and problem-solving.

Older Isn't Necessarily Wiser; Younger Isn't Necessarily Innovative

In the journey of problem-solving and seeking the truth, we often encounter age-related stereotypes that can influence our perceptions of wisdom and innovation. However, it is essential to recognize that age alone does not determine the depth of wisdom or the potential for innovation.

This section delves into the misconceptions surrounding age and highlights the importance of evaluating individuals based on their unique qualities and contributions.

Dispelling the Age-Related Myths is important. Wisdom is not solely the domain of the older generation; it can be found across all age groups. Innovation thrives in individuals of all ages, not limited to the younger generation.

Embracing Diverse Perspectives involves encouraging an inclusive environment that values the insights of people of all ages and recognizing the different life experiences that contribute to unique perspectives. The *Value of Experience and Continual Learning* shows that experience can provide valuable insights and lessons learned over time, emphasizing the importance of ongoing learning and adapting to new challenges.

Nurturing Innovation and Creativity requires fostering a culture that promotes innovation and creativity across all age groups and creating platforms where ideas can be shared and explored without age-based biases.

Breaking Stereotypes Through Collaboration means encouraging collaboration between individuals of different ages and backgrounds, leveraging the strengths of each age group to complement one another.

Empowering Individuals to Speak Up ensures that individuals of all ages feel comfortable expressing their ideas and opinions, empowering younger voices to share innovative insights while respecting the wisdom of the older generation.

Recognizing the Intersection of *Wisdom and Innovation* acknowledges that wisdom and innovation can coexist and reinforce one another, striving for a balance between drawing from experience and exploring novel approaches.

Leveraging Mentorship and Reverse Mentorship involves older individuals providing guidance and mentorship to younger counterparts, while younger individuals can offer fresh perspectives and tech-savvy approaches to older generations.

In the pursuit of truth and effective problem-solving, age should not be the sole factor in evaluating someone's wisdom or innovative capabilities. By breaking free from age-related stereotypes, fostering a culture of inclusivity, and embracing diverse perspectives, we can tap into the collective power of different age groups.

Wisdom gained through experience and the innovative spirit of the younger generation are not mutually exclusive; instead, they can combine to form a potent force for positive change.

19. Dealing With Personality

In the journey of problem-solving and interacting with others, one essential aspect is the ability to set aside one's ego.

Ego can be a significant roadblock to effective communication and cooperation, often hindering the progress of finding solutions to various challenges.

To truly embrace problem-solving and work harmoniously with others, individuals must learn to tame their egos and foster a more constructive and open-minded approach.

- **Recognizing the Ego**: The first step in dealing with one's ego is recognizing its presence. Ego can manifest in various ways, such as being overly defensive about one's ideas, seeking constant validation, or being resistant to feedback and criticism. By being aware of these tendencies, individuals can begin to understand how their ego may impact their problem-solving process.

- **Embracing Humility**: Humility plays a vital role in setting aside one's ego. Understanding that everyone has limitations and room for growth enables individuals to approach problem-solving with a willingness to learn from others. Embracing humility creates an atmosphere of mutual respect, where ideas and perspectives can be shared freely.

- **Active Listening**: One of the most effective ways to set aside ego during problem-solving is to practice active listening. Often, the desire to assert one's ideas can lead to interrupting or dismissing others. Active listening involves giving full attention to the speaker, valuing their input, and refraining from immediate judgment or rebuttal.

- **Valuing Collaboration**: Problem-solving is seldom a solo endeavor. Emphasizing the value of collaboration over individual accomplishments encourages a collective effort towards finding solutions. Acknowledging that diverse viewpoints can enrich the problem-solving process helps create a positive and inclusive environment.

- **Constructive Feedback**: Providing and receiving feedback is essential for personal growth and effective problem-solving. However, the ego might resist feedback as it can feel like a personal attack. Learning to accept feedback gracefully and offering constructive feedback to others without criticism fosters a culture of continuous improvement.

- **Celebrating Successes Together**: Rather than seeking personal glory, focus on celebrating successes as a team. Recognizing and appreciating each team member's contributions creates a sense of unity and encourages a healthy team dynamic. Shared achievements lead to stronger bonds and motivate individuals to keep setting their egos aside for the greater good.

In the pursuit of effective problem-solving, setting aside one's ego is a crucial skill to develop. It allows individuals to approach challenges with a clear and open mind, value diverse perspectives, and collaborate more effectively with others.

By practicing humility, active listening, and constructive feedback, individuals can create an environment where problem-solving becomes a collective effort, leading to more innovative and successful outcomes. Remember, it's not about suppressing one's individuality, but rather, channeling it in a way that benefits the team and the ultimate goal of finding solutions.

Letting Others Take The Credit

In the realm of problem-solving and teamwork, an essential quality to cultivate is the willingness to let others take the credit. While recognition for one's efforts is undoubtedly gratifying, true collaboration and a harmonious work environment thrive when individuals prioritize the success of the team over personal acclaim.

Sometimes it's a group effort and other times it's an individual standout. Be willing to share the glory. After all, they may well deserve it more!

- **Shifting the Focus to Team Success**: Instead of seeking personal recognition, individuals should focus on the collective success of the team. Acknowledging and celebrating the contributions of others, especially when they lead to positive outcomes, fosters a supportive atmosphere and strengthens team camaraderie.

- **Understanding the Power of Recognition**: Recognizing the efforts of team members, even if it means letting them take the credit, creates a culture of appreciation and motivation. When individuals feel valued and acknowledged for their hard work, they become more engaged and committed to the group's goals.

- **Trust and Delegation**: Letting others take the credit requires a level of trust in the abilities of one's teammates. Delegating tasks and responsibilities with confidence demonstrates respect for their skills and expertise. This, in turn, encourages a sense of empowerment and accountability among team members.

- **Collaboration over Competition**: Fostering a collaborative environment, rather than a competitive one, is essential for effective problem-solving. When individuals work together selflessly and put the team's interests above their own, the focus shifts from personal gain to achieving collective excellence.

- **Being Generous with Praise**: Compliment and praise others for their hard work and achievements sincerely. A culture of generosity with praise and recognition creates a positive and motivating atmosphere, encouraging team members to continue contributing their best efforts.

- **Leading by Deflecting**: Leaders play a critical role in shaping the team's culture. When leaders actively let others take the credit and appreciate their team's achievements, they set a positive example for everyone else to follow. This creates a ripple effect, encouraging others to do the same.

If someone offers credit to you for a team accomplishment, learn to deflect it gracefully when appropriate. Acknowledge your role in the project but also highlight the significant contributions of others. Redirect the attention to the team's collective efforts rather than solely focusing on individual contributions.

- **Leading by Example**: Finding fulfillment in contributing to the team's success and witnessing the growth of others can be more rewarding than personal accolades. Letting others take the credit becomes an opportunity for personal growth, as it teaches individuals to derive satisfaction from their positive impact on the team and the organization as a whole.

  As a leader or influential team member, lead by example and exemplify the value of letting others take the credit. Demonstrate humility and selflessness in acknowledging the efforts of team members and give credit where it is due. Your actions will set the tone for the entire team.

Letting others take the credit is not about diminishing one's value or accomplishments. Instead, it is a powerful demonstration of selflessness, trust, and teamwork.

In the collaborative landscape of problem-solving, recognizing the achievements of others fosters an environment where every team member feels appreciated and motivated. By prioritizing team success over individual recognition, individuals can contribute to a more harmonious and effective problem-solving process.

Remember, when everyone is willing to share the credit, the team's accomplishments become a testament to the collective strength of its members.

Taking and Assigning Blame

In the complex landscape of problem-solving, both taking and assigning blame play crucial roles in the success of large projects. However, the order in which these actions occur is essential.

First and foremost, individuals must embrace the responsibility of accepting blame collectively, fostering an environment where team members feel safe to acknowledge their mistakes without fear of reprisal.

Only after establishing this culture of accountability can the process of assigning blame be approached constructively and fairly.

- **Taking Blame**: Accepting blame is an act of courage and maturity. When something goes wrong within a project, individuals should be willing to take responsibility for their part in the situation, even if it was unintentional.

  By holding themselves accountable, team members demonstrate integrity and a commitment to learning and improvement. Taking blame should not be seen as a sign of weakness, but rather as a demonstration of personal growth and a dedication to the project's overall success.

- **Cultivating a Blame-Free Culture**: In large projects, it is crucial to cultivate a blame-free culture where team members can openly discuss errors and challenges without fear of harsh judgment or punishment.

  When the focus shifts from finding a scapegoat to understanding the root cause of problems, teams can learn from their mistakes and implement effective solutions. A blame-free culture encourages transparency, open communication, and a collective desire to learn and grow.

- **Learning from Mistakes**: Instead of dwelling on mistakes and pointing fingers, the emphasis should be on learning from them. Analyzing the factors that led to an issue allows the team to identify areas for improvement and implement preventive measures.

  Taking blame serves as an opportunity for personal and team development, enabling a more resilient and adaptable approach to problem-solving.

- **Assigning Blame Fairly**: Once a culture of accountability has been established, and the focus is on learning from mistakes, the process of assigning blame can be carried out more effectively. It is essential to approach this task with objectivity and fairness.

  Blame should be based on a thorough assessment of the facts and should not target individuals in a punitive manner. Instead, the aim is to understand the chain of events that led to the problem and to hold accountable those whose actions or decisions contributed to the issue.

- **Encouraging Collective Responsibility**: In assigning blame, it is crucial to remember that large projects often involve numerous interdependent tasks and team members.

  Encouraging collective responsibility ensures that everyone involved reflects on their role in the project's outcome. Instead of singling out individuals, the focus should be on fostering a sense of collective ownership and commitment to success.

In the realm of large project problem-solving, taking blame and assigning blame are intertwined elements that must be approached thoughtfully.

Accepting blame establishes a foundation of accountability and personal growth within the team.

In a blame-free culture, mistakes are viewed as opportunities for learning and improvement rather than sources of shame or punishment.

When assigning blame, objectivity and fairness are paramount, with the ultimate goal of identifying areas for improvement and encouraging collective responsibility.

Embracing these principles, teams can navigate the challenges of large projects more effectively, creating an atmosphere of trust, collaboration, and continuous improvement.

Dealing With Personality Conflicts

In any collaborative environment, personality conflicts are almost inevitable. When individuals with diverse backgrounds, experiences, and communication styles come together to work on a project, clashes can arise.

However, the ability to manage and resolve personality conflicts is crucial for maintaining a harmonious and productive team. By addressing these conflicts with empathy, effective communication, and a willingness to find common ground, teams can transform challenging situations into opportunities for growth and improved collaboration.

- **Recognizing the Signs of Personality Conflicts**: The first step in dealing with personality conflicts is to recognize their presence.

  Signs of personality conflicts may include frequent arguments, tension during discussions, passive-aggressive behavior, or even avoidance of certain team members. Being attentive to these signs allows teams to address conflicts proactively before they escalate further.

- **Encourage Open Communication**: Create an environment where team members feel comfortable expressing their concerns and emotions openly. Encourage active listening and respect for differing viewpoints. When team members feel heard and understood, it becomes easier to identify the root causes of conflicts and work towards resolution.

- **Seek to Understand**: Take the time to understand each team member's personality, communication style, and motivations. Often, conflicts arise from misunderstandings or misinterpretations. By seeking to understand each other's perspectives, team members can build empathy and find common ground for resolving conflicts.

- **Mediation and Facilitation**: In more complex personality conflicts, consider involving a neutral third party to mediate and facilitate discussions.

  A mediator can help create a safe space for team members to express themselves and guide the conversation towards constructive solutions. Having an impartial mediator can prevent conflicts from becoming personal and allow for more objective problem-solving.

- **Focus on the Task at Hand**: During conflicts, it's easy to get caught up in personal disagreements and lose sight of the project's objectives. Remind team members to keep the focus on the task at hand and the larger goal they are working towards. Redirecting attention to the project's success can help minimize the intensity of personality conflicts.

- **Implement Conflict Resolution Strategies**: Establish conflict resolution strategies within the team to address conflicts as they arise. These strategies might include taking a break to cool off before discussing issues, using "I" statements to express feelings, finding compromises, or engaging in team-building exercises. Having predefined approaches to handle conflicts fosters a proactive and solution-oriented team culture.

- **Emphasize Collaboration and Respect**: Promote a culture of collaboration and mutual respect within the team. Encourage team members to value each other's contributions and acknowledge the strengths that each individual brings to the project. By celebrating diversity and fostering a sense of camaraderie, personality conflicts are less likely to escalate.

Dealing with personality conflicts is an inherent part of any team environment. Rather than seeing conflicts as destructive forces, teams can view them as opportunities for growth and improvement.

By recognizing the signs of conflicts, promoting open communication, seeking to understand one another, and implementing conflict resolution strategies, teams can navigate personality conflicts effectively.

Emphasizing collaboration and respect within the team helps create a supportive and cohesive working environment, enabling team members to harness their diverse perspectives and skills to overcome challenges and achieve shared success.

Remember, conflicts are a natural part of human interactions, and handling them constructively can lead to stronger, more resilient teams.

20. Leadership

In the realm of problem-solving, leadership plays an indispensable role. Effective leadership is not merely about giving directives; it's about cultivating an environment where challenges are not shunned but embraced.

Leaders, with their foresight and vision, have the capacity to frame problems in ways that not only delineate the issue but also inspire and galvanize their teams towards actionable solutions.

By articulating the significance of the problem and presenting it as an opportunity for growth, leaders can ignite a collective passion and determination in their teams to navigate complexities and arrive at innovative solutions.

Moreover, an adept leader recognizes the strength in diversity, championing open communication and encouraging varied perspectives. This inclusivity ensures a comprehensive understanding of the problem and promotes a holistic approach to finding solutions.

A good leader listens, assimilates feedback, and delegates tasks based on individual strengths, ensuring every facet of the problem is addressed efficiently.

By fostering a culture of trust, respect, and mutual support, leaders drive not just problem-solving, but also team growth and cohesion, making the journey as significant as the solution itself.

Don't Ask Someone To Do Something You Wouldn't Do Yourself

The adage "Don't ask someone to do something you wouldn't do yourself" stands as a testament to empathetic and effective leadership.

This principle is not about a leader being capable of performing every task, but rather understanding the magnitude and intricacies of what they're asking of their team members.

By placing themselves in the shoes of their subordinates, leaders can gauge the feasibility of tasks, ensuring that they're neither overwhelming nor demoralizing.

This approach fosters respect and trust, as team members recognize their leader's awareness and consideration of their capacities and boundaries.

In the realm of problem-solving, this principle plays a crucial role. When leaders hand off challenges, it's essential that they understand the complexity and effort required to address them.
By ensuring that problems are assigned based on an individual's skill set, experience, and capacity, leaders optimize the chances of successful resolution.

Assigning problems that are mismatched to an individual's capabilities can lead to frustration, decreased morale, and inefficient problem-solving processes.

On the other hand, appropriately scaled challenges can empower team members, offering them opportunities for growth and showcasing their expertise.

Furthermore, this principle underscores the importance of leaders being role models. By demonstrating a willingness to tackle challenges head-on and not shying away from difficult tasks, leaders set a standard of dedication, resilience, and accountability.

This proactive attitude sends a powerful message about the organization's values and work ethic. When team members see their leaders taking on challenges and demonstrating tenacity, they are more inclined to mirror those behaviors, fostering a culture where problems are addressed with enthusiasm and commitment.

Example: Marissa, the Tech Lead

Marissa was the Tech Lead of a growing software development team. Their newest project was to integrate a complex AI algorithm into their software to help users automate some tasks. She had previously worked on similar integrations and knew the challenges involved: long hours of coding, rigorous testing phases, and potential issues in matching the new algorithm with the existing software infrastructure.

When the project started, Marissa had a choice. She could delegate the entire task to James, a promising but relatively new developer on her team, or she could involve herself directly, collaborating and sharing the workload.

Marissa chose to take the lead on the initial stages of the integration. She wanted to understand firsthand any major issues that might arise and ensure that the project's foundational steps were solid. As she worked, she documented challenges, solutions, and insights.

Once she felt the ground was steady, she involved James, guiding him through the complexities she had encountered. This not only made James's task more manageable but also served as a learning experience.

James appreciated Marissa's hands-on approach and mentorship, and he felt more confident tackling the tasks assigned to him. He knew that Marissa wouldn't give him something she hadn't tried or understood herself.

As a result, the integration process went smoother than expected. The team lauded Marissa's leadership style, and James felt empowered, having been given a challenge that was demanding yet achievable with the right guidance.

Identifying Your Own Leadership Faults (and correcting them)

Leadership, while often seen as a position of strength and guidance, requires a continuous journey of introspection and growth. Most leaders are adept at recognizing and addressing their pronounced weaknesses, but it's the rare, overlooked faults that can be the most detrimental.

These nuanced imperfections often fly under the radar, manifesting subtly in decision-making processes, team interactions, and overall leadership approach.

They might not cause immediate disruption, but over time, their cumulative effects can erode trust, stifle innovation, and hamper team morale.

The challenge lies in identifying these latent faults, as they're typically interwoven with a leader's strengths. For instance, a leader's ability to make quick decisions – a seemingly positive trait – might mask an underlying impulsiveness or reluctance to consider alternative perspectives.

To uncover and address these faults, leaders must cultivate a culture of feedback, seeking honest input from peers, mentors, and team members alike.

Anonymous feedback mechanisms, periodic self-reflection, and engaging in leadership training or coaching can be invaluable. Once identified, the key is not just acknowledgment, but active rectification.

This might involve retraining oneself, altering decision-making frameworks, or even seeking mentorship on specific issues. By addressing these rare faults head-on, leaders not only enhance their efficacy but also set a precedent of humility, growth, and continuous improvement within their teams.

Identifying Leadership Flaws In Others

Identifying leadership flaws in others is a nuanced task that requires both empathy and analytical skills. While every leader has a unique style, and what works for one may not work for another, certain universal flaws can hinder a leader's effectiveness and the success of their team.

One common flaw is a lack of clear communication. Leaders who are unable to articulate their vision, goals, or expectations can inadvertently create confusion and uncertainty within their teams. This might manifest in team members frequently seeking clarity, projects stalling due to unclear directives, or a general sense of disorganization.

Another notable flaw is an inability or unwillingness to adapt to change. In our rapidly evolving world, adaptability is a key leadership trait. Leaders who cling rigidly to old methods or who dismiss new ideas without consideration can stifle innovation and hinder the growth and adaptability of their team.

Furthermore, a lack of emotional intelligence can be a significant flaw. Leaders who cannot empathize with their team members, or who react impulsively rather than responding thoughtfully, can erode trust and damage team morale.

It's not just about understanding emotions; it's about managing and channeling them effectively in interpersonal interactions.

However, when identifying flaws in others, it's crucial to approach the subject with care and constructive intent.

Labeling and criticizing without offering solutions or support can be counterproductive. Instead, focusing on understanding the underlying causes of the flaws and facilitating a growth mindset can lead to positive change and strengthened leadership capabilities.

Example: Jackson and the Weekly Team Meetings

At SolarTech Enterprises, the weekly team meetings led by Jackson, a department head, were often a source of dread for his team. Jackson was known for his technical expertise and had been with the company for over a decade.

However, there were clear leadership flaws that came to light during these sessions.

Jackson's meetings were typically unstructured. He would jump from topic to topic without a clear agenda, leading to confusion. Team members often left the meetings unsure of their tasks or priorities for the week. This reflected a lack of clear communication, a common leadership flaw.

Additionally, Jackson would often dismiss new ideas or methodologies without due consideration, immediately reverting to "how things have always been done." This resistance to change left younger team members, eager to innovate, feeling unheard and stifled.

However, it was his lack of emotional intelligence that became the tipping point. In one meeting, a team member, Lara, proposed a new software tool to streamline their workflow. Rather than considering its merits or providing constructive feedback, Jackson curtly shot it down with a comment about "unnecessary complications."

Lara, who had spent weeks researching and testing the tool, felt demoralized and undervalued.

Observing these recurring issues, a senior manager, Naomi, decided to intervene. Recognizing Jackson's value to the company but also the importance of effective leadership, she organized a series of leadership training workshops.

The workshops focused on clear communication, adaptability, and emotional intelligence. With time and guidance, Jackson started to recognize and work on his flaws. The weekly meetings became more organized, and he began to listen more actively to his team's suggestions.

By addressing Jackson's leadership flaws, SolarTech not only improved team morale and efficiency but also fostered a culture of continuous growth and learning.

Great Leadership Traits

Leadership is multifaceted, and while different situations may require different leadership approaches, there are certain traits that are commonly recognized as beneficial for effective leadership across various contexts.

Here are ten of the most universally valued leadership traits:

1. **Vision**: Great leaders have a clear, long-term vision of where they want to go and can articulate that vision in an inspiring way. This helps set direction and unify teams around a common purpose.

2. **Integrity**: Trust is foundational in leadership, and it's built on consistently demonstrating honesty and strong moral principles. Leaders with integrity stand by their word and their values.

3. **Emotional Intelligence (EQ)**: Effective leaders can recognize, understand, and manage their own emotions while also empathizing with and influencing the emotions of those around them. This aids in building strong interpersonal relationships.

4. **Adaptability**: In our ever-changing world, the ability to adapt to new situations and challenges, especially during times of crisis, is crucial. This means being open to feedback and willing to change course when necessary.

5. **Decision-Making Capabilities**: Leaders frequently need to make difficult decisions, sometimes with limited information. Strong decision-makers analyze available data, consider team input, and then commit with confidence.

6. **Empathy**: Great leaders understand and care about the feelings and needs of others. This trait builds trust, encourages open communication, and fosters a positive team environment.

7. **Resilience**: The capacity to recover quickly from difficulties and setbacks is vital. Leaders will inevitably face challenges, but it's their ability to bounce back and lead their team through adversity that sets them apart.

8. **Effective Communication**: Beyond just conveying information, effective leaders ensure their message is understood. They also listen actively, valuing input from all team members.

9. **Delegation and Empowerment**: Recognizing that they cannot do everything alone, successful leaders delegate tasks to the right individuals and trust them to execute. This not only frees up the leader's time but also empowers team members, fostering growth and development.

10. **Continuous Learning**: The best leaders understand that there's always room for improvement. They seek out learning opportunities, stay updated with industry trends, and encourage a culture of continuous personal and professional growth.

These traits, while inherently valuable, become even more potent when combined. Leaders who embody multiple or all of these qualities are better positioned to inspire their teams, drive results, and leave a lasting positive impact.

21. Managing Limited Resources and Setting Priorities

In the realm of problem-solving, the idyllic scenario often conjured is one where managers possess an abundance of resources—endless funding, limitless time, and an assembly of unparalleled talents at their beck and call.

In this dreamlike world, obstacles vanish, challenges bow before the sheer might of resources, and solutions flow effortlessly.

However, reality rarely extends such luxuries. The pragmatic landscape of problem-solving is frequently marked by constraints, the most formidable of which are the limitations of resources.

Time, that elusive and non-renewable asset, steadily marches forward. Budgets, though carefully allocated, remain finite, and the pool of available skills and talents is not inexhaustible.

Yet, it's within these constraints that the true art of problem-solving emerges. The mark of a skilled manager lies not in the ability to conjure resources from thin air, but in the capacity to craft effective solutions within the bounds of what's available. This requires not only astute decision-making but also a discerning eye for setting priorities.

Navigating the complex tapestry of limited resources is akin to sculpting a masterpiece from a finite block of stone. Each chisel mark must be deliberate, every stroke of effort purposeful.

To achieve this, understanding the problem at its core is imperative. It's the compass that guides the allocation of precious resources.

Within this challenge lies the art of setting priorities. Like a conductor orchestrating an intricate symphony, a manager must harmonize the disparate elements of time, budget, and talent.

Decisions must be made on what to emphasize, what to delegate, and what to forgo. The conductor must choose the most impactful notes to play in the grand composition of problem-solving.

When Success Brings Its Own Challenges

In the realm of business, there's a dream that many aspire to but few are fully prepared for - the dream of having too many customers. It's a scenario where success surges beyond expectations, and a wave of clients, customers, or users pours in.

On the surface, it seems like an enviable predicament, a testament to a product or service's undeniable appeal. However, beneath the surface, it brings its own unique set of challenges, one of the most pressing being the scarcity of talent to meet the demands of this surging success.

A Bounty of Customers, a Dearth of Talent

When success knocks with unexpected intensity, an organization can find itself walking a tightrope. The influx of demand may outstrip the capacity of the workforce. As orders pile up and service requests multiply, it becomes evident that while there are plenty of customers eager to engage, there are not enough skilled hands to serve them.

The Challenges of Managing Abundance

This scenario might seem paradoxical - the abundance of customers should ideally translate into a wealth of resources. However, it's a stark reminder that success, while a worthy pursuit, must be managed wisely. Here are some challenges associated with this predicament:

Quality vs. Quantity: Balancing the desire to serve all customers with maintaining the quality of service is a critical challenge. Rushed or subpar services can erode the very success that brought in the customers in the first place.

Recruitment and Training: Rapidly expanding a workforce is not always feasible or advisable. Rushed hiring can lead to issues of competency and culture fit. Effective training takes time and resources.

Resource Allocation: Deciding which customers or projects to prioritize becomes a crucial dilemma. Not every opportunity can be seized simultaneously, and decisions must align with the organization's strategic goals.

Sustainability: Temporary bursts of success can be followed by equally sudden downturns. Preparing for the long term while dealing with short-term abundance is a balancing act.

The Art of Prioritization in Abundance

In the face of too many customers and not enough talent, the art of setting priorities becomes paramount. It involves the careful selection of which opportunities to pursue and which to defer.

Prioritizing customers or projects that align with long-term goals and ensuring that the quality of service is maintained becomes crucial.

Success, while a double-edged sword, can also be a crucible for innovation and growth. It forces organizations to refine their strategies, invest in talent development, and adopt scalable solutions.

Navigating Capacity Constraints

In the intricate dance of problem-solving within the business world, the limitations of capacity often loom large.

Whether it's the physical confines of office space, the number of skilled personnel at your disposal, or the availability of essential equipment, the concept of capacity is a pivotal factor that can either empower or constrain your endeavors.

The Space Conundrum

Office space, while seemingly mundane, can exert a significant influence on your ability to execute projects and serve clients. In bustling urban landscapes, securing sufficient space can be both a logistical challenge and a financial strain.

When your operations outgrow your physical confines, the delicate balance between collaboration and concentration can be disrupted.

Navigating the office space dilemma requires astute resource allocation. How you design, utilize, and expand your workspace can impact not only your team's productivity but also your organization's ability to attract and retain talent.

People Power and Equipment Efficiency

People are the lifeblood of any organization, and their availability, skills, and motivation are pivotal. Having a capable and committed workforce is a cornerstone of success.

However, there are times when you find yourself with more tasks than hands to perform them. Talent acquisition and retention strategies become essential in such scenarios.

Likewise, the availability of equipment and technology can be a bottleneck. Outdated or inadequate tools can hinder progress, while the strategic allocation of resources toward the latest technologies can provide a competitive edge.

Example: Taming the Laundry List of Enhancements

In the world of problem-solving and project management, it's not uncommon to encounter a laundry list of potential enhancements and improvements.

These lists, often brimming with ideas and opportunities, can be both a blessing and a curse. While they reflect a desire for growth and progress, they can also become unwieldy, especially when resources are limited.

The Perils of Quantity Over Quality

The challenge arises when organizations strive to tackle every item on these lists without considering the capacity and priority of each enhancement.

Often, this results in a situation where the quantity of lower-priority items prevents the allocation of resources to more critical endeavors.

It's akin to a restaurant trying to introduce dozens of new dishes to its menu without ensuring that each one is perfected. The result can be a dilution of effort, leading to mediocrity across the board instead of excellence in a select few.

Prioritization as the North Star

To address this issue effectively, prioritization becomes the North Star. It involves carefully evaluating each enhancement, considering factors like potential impact, alignment with strategic objectives, and available resources.

Some questions to ponder include: Which enhancements are mission-critical? Which ones offer the most significant return on investment? Which align best with the organization's long-term vision? By focusing resources on a select few high-priority enhancements, organizations can channel their energy and expertise into making meaningful strides.

Additionally, adopting a structured approach, such as the Eisenhower Matrix (which categorizes tasks into four quadrants based on urgency and importance), can be invaluable.

It helps teams categorize enhancements into "Do First," "Schedule," "Delegate," or "Don't Do" categories, providing clarity on where resources should be directed and where they can be deferred or discarded.

Controlling the Purse Strings

In the intricate dance of problem-solving within organizations, one of the most vital roles often falls to those who control the purse strings—the financial decision-makers.

Effective resource management and prioritization hinge on the judicious allocation of funds, and those who hold this responsibility play a pivotal role in determining the path an organization will take.

The Power of Financial Control

Controlling the purse strings is akin to holding the reins of a mighty steed. It's the ability to steer the organization in the desired direction, fueling the projects and initiatives deemed most strategic and valuable.

In a world of limited resources, financial decision-makers must navigate a complex landscape, making choices that align with the organization's goals and deliver the highest return on investment.

Balancing Innovation and Prudence

The challenge lies in striking a balance between innovation and prudence. On one hand, investments must be made to drive growth and keep pace with a dynamic marketplace.

On the other, fiscal responsibility is essential to maintain stability and safeguard against unexpected downturns. Financial decision-makers must weigh the potential benefits of each investment against the available resources and the organization's financial health.

Effective Collaboration

To succeed in controlling the purse strings, collaboration is key. It's not a solitary endeavor but a collective effort that involves aligning financial decisions with the priorities set by the organization's leadership and project managers. Effective communication channels must be established to ensure that resources are allocated to the right projects and that everyone is working towards common objectives.

22. Probability of Random Numbers

In the vast world of probability, there lies a fundamental distinction between what is "possible" and what is "probable."

At first glance, these terms might appear synonymous, but when delving deeper into the intricacies of chance and randomness, their differences become starkly clear.

Consider the simple act of flipping a coin. For most practical intents, we acknowledge two outcomes: heads or tails. This binary result is what we often base our probabilistic calculations on, assigning a 50% chance for each side.

But, if we were to scrutinize the scenario further, we'd recognize a third potential outcome: the coin landing on its edge. While this event is technically possible, its occurrence is so rare that it's almost negligible in common discussions of coin-flipping odds.

To bring the distinction between "probable" and "possible" into clearer focus, think of the "possible" as the universe of all potential outcomes, including the most bizarre and unlikely ones.

In contrast, the "probable" hones in on the outcomes that are more likely to happen, given a set of conditions or over numerous trials. In our coin example, it's possible for the coin to land on its edge, but it's far more probable for it to land as either heads or tails.

Understanding this differentiation is crucial for effective problem-solving. While it's essential to recognize all possible outcomes (to account for outliers or rare events), it's often more practical to focus on the probable scenarios when making decisions or predictions.

This allows for a more efficient use of resources, a clearer understanding of risks, and a streamlined approach to tackling challenges.

The game of roulette offers another illustrative example of the distinction between "probable" and "possible." On a standard American roulette wheel, there are 38 pockets: 18 red, 18 black, and 2 green (the single 0 and the double 00). Players can place bets on various outcomes, ranging from specific numbers to color groups.

If we were to spin the wheel, any one of these 38 pockets is a *possible* outcome; the ball has the potential to land in any of them. However, not all these outcomes are equally *probable*.

For instance, if you were to bet on the ball landing in a green pocket, the probability of this happening is 2 out of 38, or approximately 5.26%. This is in stark contrast to betting on red or black, where the probability jumps to 18 out of 38, or about 47.37%.

Here's where the concept of "probable versus possible" comes into play. It's certainly *possible* for the ball to land on the single 0 or double 00 on any given spin, but over many spins, it's more *probable* for the ball to land on red or black pockets simply because there are more of them.

A player should understand this distinction when placing bets. While hitting a green pocket might offer a higher payout due to its lower probability, the chances of this occurring are less than those of landing on red or black.

The Rarity of Infinitesimal Occurrences: Is It Worth Designing For?

In the realm of problem-solving, one often encounters a plethora of potential solutions, some of which account for situations that are exceedingly rare.

These are the outliers, the exceptions, the 'black swan' events that, while possible, are buried deep within the tail ends of a probability curve.

As the number of potential outcomes increases, especially in complex systems or situations, there may indeed be an infinite number of these possibilities. The crucial question then arises: Is it worth designing for such rare events?

From a purely statistical standpoint, it might seem wasteful or even counterproductive to design solutions around occurrences that are almost infinitesimal in their probability.

Allocating resources, time, and effort to cater to these rarities can detract from focusing on more common and probable scenarios that are more likely to manifest. In many contexts, it's more efficient and practical to design systems that handle the "middle" of the bell curve rather than its extreme tails.

However, the counterargument lies in the potential impact of these rare events. Some events, though improbable, can carry catastrophic consequences if they do occur.

For instance, in engineering or safety-critical domains, the failure to account for a one-in-a-million event could lead to significant harm or loss. In such cases, the severity of the potential outcome justifies the investment in preventive or mitigative measures, even if the event is unlikely.

Considering Earthquake Risk in Unlikely Locations: A Lesson in Preparedness

When contemplating risks in geographical regions, it's easy to dismiss certain natural disasters based on historical data and common wisdom. Earthquakes serve as a prominent example.

There are well-known seismic hotspots around the world where earthquakes are frequent and expected.

However, there are also locations where earthquakes are so rare that they're hardly a blip on the radar of local concerns. The question is: should these regions ignore the risk, or take it into account when planning and building?

At first glance, it may seem unnecessary, even economically imprudent, to design earthquake-resistant structures in an area where earthquakes have historically been rare or nonexistent.

After all, doing so would involve higher construction costs, more stringent regulations, and perhaps even a redirection of resources from other more immediate concerns. However, just because something is rare doesn't mean it's impossible.

Let's consider the worst-case scenario: an unexpected earthquake strikes a region unprepared for it. Buildings, infrastructure, and homes not designed to withstand seismic activity could suffer significant damage. The cost, both in terms of monetary value and potential loss of life, could be astronomical.

What's even more tragic about such a situation is that the damage and loss could have been mitigated or even prevented with proper foresight and planning.

In more extreme cases, a single rare event could lead to catastrophic losses, obliterating years of economic growth and development. The repercussions can extend beyond just the immediate aftermath, affecting the region's socio-economic fabric for generations.

It becomes a stark reminder that sometimes, the potential magnitude of an outcome should take precedence over its likelihood.

"Math is Math is Math": The Power of Precision in Risk Assessment

In the realm of problem-solving, there's an oft-repeated mantra that underscores the undeniable truth and precision of numerical analysis: "Math is math is math."

At its core, this statement serves as a reminder of the unwavering reliability of mathematical computation, especially when navigating the murky waters of risk and probability.

In many scenarios, particularly those involving rare events and minimal risks, mathematics can provide clarity, enabling decision-makers to optimize efforts and resources efficiently.

Imagine a situation where an event's occurrence is so rare that its probability is less than 0.1%.

If we combine this with the knowledge that, even if this event did occur, its consequences would be negligible, we find ourselves facing a conundrum. Is it worth diverting significant resources to guard against such an improbable event? This is where the power of mathematics shines.

By running precise calculations, we can quantify the risk in concrete terms. Let's say the potential damage of our rare event is valued at $10,000.

Multiplying this by the 0.1% likelihood of occurrence gives us an "expected loss" of $10.

Now, if mitigating this risk entirely costs $1,000, the math makes it clear: spending ten times the expected loss to prevent it is not a cost-effective decision. On the other hand, if a solution exists that mitigates the risk for just $5, then it becomes a worthwhile investment.

This methodical, mathematical approach allows for a clear distinction between necessary precautions and over-preparation. While it's tempting to aim for a 100% foolproof solution, it's often neither feasible nor economical.

By working the numbers, one can often find that a 99.9% solution is not only sufficient but also the most efficient and logical choice. It's about balancing the ideal with the practical.

In the end, while human intuition and judgment are invaluable assets in problem-solving, there are instances where the unemotional, unerring precision of mathematics offers the clearest guidance.

When "math is math is math," it provides a compass by which we can navigate uncertainty with confidence.

23. Listening

In the hustle and bustle of today's fast-paced world, many have become entranced with the sound of their own voices.

We often assume that leadership means dominating the conversation, laying out plans, and offering a barrage of directives. However, in doing so, leaders may inadvertently close themselves off to valuable insights and feedback.

It's not hard to see why. Speaking gives a sense of control, a platform to express ideas and exert influence. But when one monopolizes the dialogue, it shifts from a two-way street of mutual understanding to a one-way broadcast.

This is especially detrimental in problem-solving scenarios. Without pausing to listen, leaders risk missing out on diverse perspectives and innovative solutions that may exist outside their immediate purview.

The art of listening is more than just the act of being silent while another speaks. It involves genuine curiosity, open-mindedness, and the patience to understand the underlying sentiments being conveyed.

By prioritizing listening, leaders not only show respect to their team members but also position themselves to receive a wealth of knowledge and advice that could prove invaluable.

In essence, true leadership doesn't equate to the volume of words spoken but rather the quality of understanding achieved. As the adage goes, we have two ears and one mouth for a reason: to listen twice as much as we speak.

Twain's Timeless Wisdom on Silence

Mark Twain, one of the most celebrated authors and humorists of his time, once wisely quipped, "It is better to keep your mouth closed and let people think you are a fool than to open it and remove all doubt." This age-old sentiment is not merely a witty observation, but a profound piece of advice, particularly for those in leadership positions.

Leaders often feel the pressure to have all the answers, believing that any display of uncertainty might be perceived as a weakness.

However, the reality is that no single individual, no matter how brilliant, can be an expert on every topic. There are moments when those in leadership roles find themselves in rooms with individuals who may have deeper expertise or fresher insights about a particular subject.

In such situations, the wisdom in Twain's words becomes particularly evident. By speaking without full knowledge, leaders not only risk misinforming their teams but also diminishing their own credibility.

True leadership isn't about always having the answers but recognizing when to speak and when to listen. In moments of uncertainty, it can be a sign of strength to pause, listen, and learn from those with more expertise.

By doing so, leaders not only enrich their own understanding but also foster an environment where every team member feels valued and heard.

In the end, it's not about avoiding looking like a fool, but rather embracing the humility and wisdom of recognizing one's own limitations and the strengths of those around them.

Stifling Opinions and Its Ripple Effect

In many organizations, there exists a paradoxical challenge: leaders who are so authoritative or vocal that they inadvertently stifle the very innovation they seek.

When a leader consistently dominates conversations or interacts with such intensity that it borders on aggression, they risk creating an atmosphere of intimidation.

In such an environment, team members, even those with brilliant ideas, may find themselves retreating into silence, fearing criticism or simply not finding an opening to share their thoughts.

This phenomenon is not merely about overtalking; it's about the atmosphere that's created. When people feel their opinions aren't valued or that they might face undue criticism, they begin to self-censor.

This self-imposed silence deprives the organization of potentially groundbreaking ideas. It's a loss not only for the individual who remains unheard but for the entire team that misses out on diverse perspectives.

Balanced leadership, on the other hand, recognizes the importance of coaxing out the thoughts of those who tend to remain silent. It's about creating a safe space where every voice, whether loud or soft, feels valued.

Leaders who master this balance often employ techniques like open-ended questioning, pausing after statements to allow for input, and actively seeking out the opinions of those who haven't yet spoken.

The most innovative and successful teams are those where every member feels they have a stake in the outcomes and are encouraged to contribute their unique insights. By fostering a culture of inclusivity and active listening, leaders can tap into a reservoir of ideas, ensuring that no valuable insight is left unspoken.

Deciphering the Unsaid: The Power of Intuitive Listening

Effective communication is as much about the words spoken as it is about those left unsaid. Often, in professional and personal interactions alike, people might not articulate their thoughts precisely.

They might dance around a topic, hint at it, or even say something that seems at odds with their true feelings or intentions. For leaders, understanding this nuance is paramount.

When someone says "X" but truly means "Y", it's not always a deliberate attempt at deception. It might be a manifestation of various factors: discomfort with a topic, fear of reprisal, societal or organizational norms, or even personal insecurities.

The leader's task is to read between the lines, to tap into their emotional intelligence and grasp the underlying sentiment.

Listening, in this context, becomes an art of intuition. It involves observing non-verbal cues like body language, tone, and facial expressions. It's about recognizing patterns in behavior, in the pauses, in the hesitations.

Such intuitive listening aids leaders in asking the right follow-up questions, offering reassurances, or simply creating an environment where the individual feels safe enough to express their genuine feelings and concerns.

By attending to what's unsaid, leaders can unearth deeper concerns, innovative ideas, or potential challenges that might not have surfaced otherwise. This holistic approach to communication not only aids in more effective problem-solving but also fosters trust.

When team members realize that their leader is genuinely striving to understand them, even when they struggle to express themselves fully, it solidifies the bond of trust and collaboration.

24. Effective Communication

In our journey through problem-solving, we've come across numerous tools and techniques that are invaluable. Yet, one of the most essential tools we possess is the power of communication. But not all communication is created equal.

Imagine you're tasked with sharing a vision for a project. Would you write an exhaustive report or would you gather your team and discuss it? The choice between written and verbal communication is pivotal and varies depending on the situation.

Picture this: You've meticulously compiled data for weeks and now you need to ensure its longevity and accessibility for future reference. Here, the written form shines.

It offers a permanence that verbal exchanges can't, ensuring that everyone, irrespective of when they access it, gets the consistent information.

And let's not forget the elegance of a well-structured report, where clarity reigns supreme and where you have the luxury of refining your words to perfection.

But there's a catch. Writing, especially when aiming for utmost clarity, can be time-consuming. And once sent, you're often left waiting, sometimes agonizingly, for a response without the chance for real-time clarification.

On the flip side, imagine being in a room, brainstorming solutions to an immediate problem. You wouldn't want to wait for written reports from each member; instead, the immediacy and dynamism of verbal communication would be your ally.

The nuances of tone, the depth of emotion, and the adaptability make spoken words incredibly powerful. And there's something to be said about the personal touch it brings, binding teams together. However, without a tangible record, crucial details from a verbal exchange can evaporate from memory, and without a structured approach, even the most eloquent of speakers can sometimes leave listeners puzzled.

So, in the intricate dance of problem-solving, how do we choose between the pen and the voice? The trick is understanding the strength of each.

When precision, formality, and wide dissemination are paramount, written communication is your best bet.

But when the situation calls for immediacy, flexibility, and personal connection, let your voice lead the way.

Laying Out the Vision

Every great endeavor starts with a vision—a guiding light that illuminates the path forward. Whether you're spearheading a project, leading a team, or solving a complex problem, having a clear and compelling vision is paramount.

But what does it mean to "lay out the vision"?

Imagine you're at the base of a mountain, and the peak represents your ultimate goal. The vision is not just the acknowledgment of the peak but also the conviction of why you wish to reach it and the benefits that come from doing so. It's the bigger picture that encapsulates the essence of what you aim to achieve.

Laying out the vision means articulating this picture in a way that's both inspiring and tangible. It's about painting a vivid image of the destination while instilling a sense of purpose. This requires clarity—being explicit about what you want to accomplish.

But it's equally important to infuse passion, making the journey towards the vision as compelling as the destination itself.

However, a vision isn't a solo endeavor. Especially in problem-solving, it's crucial that everyone involved sees, understands, and buys into this vision. Communication becomes key. Whether it's through stories, analogies, or concrete plans, the vision must resonate, bridging the gap between the abstract and the actionable.

Crafting a Consistent Message

In the intricate ballet of problem-solving and communication, there exists a subtle yet powerful tool: consistency.

The realm of communication is littered with tales of projects that veered off course, not due to a lack of effort or resources, but because the message at their core wavered and wobbled, losing its potency over time.

Imagine setting sail on a vast ocean, charting a course towards a distant island. If the captain changes direction with every shift of the wind, the ship will be tossed aimlessly, and the crew will lose faith in their journey.

The same holds true for communication. A message that constantly shifts, even if only slightly, can create ripples of confusion, doubt, and mistrust.

Crafting a consistent message isn't just about repetition, but about maintaining the essence and integrity of your core message over time and across various platforms. It's an affirmation that the vision remains unchanged, even as strategies and tactics might evolve.

However, consistency doesn't mean rigidity. It's not about being unyielding or resistant to change. Rather, it's about ensuring that any adjustments made align with the foundational principles of your initial message. It's about evolution without loss of identity.

The advantages of consistent messaging are numerous and significant. It builds trust, as stakeholders come to believe in the reliability of the message and the messenger. It creates a strong brand or project identity, making it easily recognizable and memorable.

And perhaps most crucially, it ensures that the entire team, organization, or community moves in harmony, singing from the same hymn sheet.

Where challenges are dynamic and solutions multifaceted, crafting a consistent message is the compass that keeps endeavors on track. It's the unwavering beacon that, even in turbulent times, guides all efforts toward the desired outcome, ensuring that no matter the twists and turns of the journey, the destination remains clear and attainable.

Visuals and Imagery: A Picture's Profound Power

We've all heard it said that "a picture is worth a thousand words." This timeless adage holds an undeniable truth, especially in the realm of communication and problem-solving.

While words are potent and can paint vivid images in our minds, there are moments where the sheer complexity or intricacy of a subject demands a more immediate, visual representation.

Consider the vast tapestry of data we often encounter. A spreadsheet teeming with numbers, while rich in information, might not immediately convey a trend or anomaly.

However, transform that data into a graph or chart, and suddenly patterns emerge, narratives unfold, and conclusions become evident.

Visuals act as a universal language, breaking down barriers of jargon, terminology, and context. They're especially valuable in multicultural or multidisciplinary settings where shared words might be scarce but the need for understanding paramount.

And let's not forget the emotional power of visuals. While a report might explain the impact of a problem, a photograph can capture the raw, unspoken emotions, instantly evoking empathy and driving home the gravity of the situation.

This emotional connection can galvanize teams and stakeholders, creating a shared sense of purpose and urgency.

Crafting a message is undeniably an art form. Words can sketch the outlines, but visuals fill in the hues, shades, and textures, bringing the picture to life.

In complex scenarios, where the road to understanding is long and winding, visuals can serve as shortcuts, illuminating the path and making the destination clear.

Thus, in our toolkit of communication, visuals and imagery are not mere supplements but essential instruments. They bridge the gap between abstraction and understanding, ensuring that even the most intricate of problems can be seen, grasped, and ultimately, solved.

Analogies: Crafting Stories Through Mental Imagery

Dive into the vast sea of communication tools, and you'll soon discover the subtle yet potent charm of analogies.

Just as pictures provide a visual representation of an idea, analogies create mental imagery through words, translating complex concepts into familiar, relatable scenarios. They bridge the chasm between the known and the unknown, making the unfamiliar feel intimate.

Consider for a moment the power of comparing the human brain to a computer. While the intricacies of neural networks and synaptic connections might elude many, almost everyone understands the basic functions of a computer.

By drawing this parallel, the unfathomable intricacy of the brain becomes a tad more accessible, a bit more tangible.

Analogies, whether conveyed through a humorous anecdote or rooted in stark reality, serve a dual purpose. First, they simplify. They distill complex ideas into digestible nuggets, making them easier to grasp. Second, they connect. They tap into our existing knowledge and experiences, creating a sense of familiarity with new or intricate concepts.

Like a skilled painter using a palette of colors to craft a vivid landscape, analogies draw upon a spectrum of experiences and memories to paint pictures in our minds. They narrate stories, not through detailed descriptions, but by linking to pre-existing narratives we already understand.

However, it's essential to tread with care. Just as a misplaced brushstroke can alter a painting's message, a poorly chosen analogy can mislead or confuse. The best analogies are not only relatable but also accurate in capturing the essence of the concept they aim to elucidate.

Consider for a moment Abraham Lincoln's monumental task of preserving the Union during the Civil War. To many, the intricacies of political maneuvering, moral debates, and battle strategies were overwhelming.

Yet, Lincoln had a gift for distilling these complexities into relatable narratives and analogies. When discussing the importance of unity, he once remarked, "A house divided against itself cannot stand."

In this simple statement, Lincoln drew an analogy between a nation and a household, making the abstract notion of national unity tangible and immediate. The mental image of a crumbling house provided a vivid representation of the potential fate of a divided nation.

In the narrative of problem-solving, analogies are the metaphoric brushstrokes that bring color and clarity to our understanding.

They don't replace the need for in-depth knowledge but serve as gateways, inviting us into a world of deeper comprehension and insight. In essence, they're the storytellers, making even the most arcane topics come alive in the theater of our minds.

Avoiding the 1,000 Slide Deck: The Art of Concise Communication

In today's digital age, slide decks have firmly established themselves as the go-to tool for conveying ideas, strategies, and proposals. Their ability to weave visuals with words offers a dynamic platform for storytelling.

Yet, therein lies a common trap: the belief that a plethora of slides will inherently amplify our message, when in reality, it might do just the opposite.

Recall a time when you found yourself in the audience, facing a seemingly endless presentation. Each subsequent slide, while packed with information, began to erode your initial intrigue. The core message, which should have shone brightly, was overshadowed by an overload of data, charts, and text.

This paints a vivid picture of a crucial principle in effective communication: clarity paired with brevity often holds the most power. A succinct slide deck, honed to its essence, can resonate more deeply than one bursting at the seams.

To steer clear of the '1,000 slide deck' predicament, embrace the discipline of selective storytelling.

Begin by pinpointing the crux of what you wish to convey. What should the audience take away? This essence will be your guiding light. Complement your words with compelling visuals, ensuring each image enhances rather than distracts.

As you craft your presentation, be relentless in your editing. Each slide must earn its place by directly serving your core message. And before the final presentation, rehearse. This will not only help you refine your delivery but may also illuminate any areas of redundancy.

In a world awash with information, what stands out is not sheer volume but the resonance of a message. As you embark on creating your next slide deck, let the mantra of clarity and concision be your guide, ensuring your message doesn't just reach, but deeply impacts, your audience.

Communication is Often Salesmanship: Pitching Ideas with Conviction

At its core, communication is not merely about relaying facts or conveying information. It's about persuading, influencing, and, in many ways, selling an idea.

Whether we're trying to convince a colleague of a new strategy, present findings to stakeholders, or rally a team around a vision, we are, in essence, pitching. And much like in sales, the success of our pitch hinges not only on the content but on the delivery.

Imagine a salesperson presenting a product. If they merely list its features without illustrating its benefits or understanding the needs of the customer, the pitch will likely fall flat.

Similarly, when communicating, merely presenting data without weaving a narrative or addressing the interests of the audience might not yield the desired impact.

The most effective communicators, like seasoned salespeople, understand their audience. They anticipate questions, counter potential objections, and highlight benefits that resonate.

They are storytellers, crafting narratives that captivate and persuade. Their tone, body language, and choice of words all work in tandem to sell their message.

Furthermore, just as trust is paramount in sales, authenticity is crucial in communication. People are more inclined to buy into a message when it's delivered with sincerity and conviction. It's not about manipulating or deceiving; it's about passionately believing in what you're saying and presenting it in a way that connects and resonates.

So, the next time you find yourself in a position to communicate, whether in a meeting, a presentation, or a casual conversation, approach it with the mindset of a salesperson. Know your product (your message), understand your customer (your audience), and pitch with passion.

After all, every act of communication is an opportunity to inspire, motivate, and persuade. Seize it with both hands.

25. Decision-making

In the vast realm of personal and professional choices, certain decisions stand out, demanding more than just an analytical gaze. These are moments that require individuals to plant their feet firmly and make a statement with their choices.

Such decisions might pivot around major project milestones, setting an organization's direction, or influencing the trajectories of people's lives. Beyond merely selecting an option, they encapsulate the courage and conviction to stand by that choice, especially in the face of potential criticism and uncertainty.

Decisions that involve "taking a stand" are characterized by deep emotional investment. They aren't just routine; they resonate on a personal level. Choosing the fate of a project or determining the future of an employee can weigh heavily on one's conscience.

Additionally, the impact of these decisions is palpable and often under the public eye. They can define leadership styles, personal ethos, and even organizational culture. Given their impact, they can sometimes stir the pot, leading to divergent views, discussions, or even confrontations.

Navigating through the maze of such decisions begins with thorough information gathering. It's crucial to be well-informed, not waiting endlessly for every last piece of data but having enough to make a conscious choice.

Equally important is acknowledging the weight of the decision. It's only natural to feel uncertain or apprehensive, and accepting these feelings can pave the way for a more reflective decision-making journey.

While seeking insights and advice from trusted peers or mentors can be invaluable, it's vital to remember that the buck stops with the decision-maker. Trusting one's instinct, which is shaped by past experiences and core values, can often lead the way.

Once a decision is made, effective and empathetic communication becomes the key. Explaining the rationale behind the choice and understanding the perspectives and emotions of those affected can go a long way in smoothing any ruffled feathers.

Every decision, especially those that challenge us, provides an avenue for growth. Whether the outcome is positive or not, reflection is essential.

Understanding what went well, and what could have been approached differently, ensures that we are better prepared the next time we need to take a stand.

At its core, it's not just about the accuracy of the decision, but about making choices with conviction and steering through their implications with grace and integrity.

Procrastination: A Mask for Indecision

At first glance, procrastination may seem like a mere lapse in discipline or time management. Yet, digging deeper, it often reveals itself as a manifestation of indecision.

The act of delaying or avoiding tasks isn't merely about laziness; it's frequently a sign of deeper uncertainties and unresolved conflicts within an individual's mind.

Procrastination is essentially the art of postponing. But what are we really postponing? More often than not, it's making a choice.

Whether it's the decision to start a new project, respond to a challenging email, or even undertake a personal transformation, procrastination serves as a buffer, protecting us from the potential discomfort or consequences of these decisions.

Why do we equate delay with protection? The answer lies in the fear of making the wrong choice. Indecision stems from a fear of failure, a fear of judgment, or even a fear of success.

By procrastinating, individuals give themselves more time, hoping that the "right" answer will magically present itself, or that the problem or task will somehow resolve or diminish on its own.

This mindset, however, is a trap. While temporary avoidance might provide a brief respite from anxiety, it often compounds the underlying issue. Tasks pile up, decisions become even more daunting, and the cycle of procrastination perpetuates, reinforcing the indecision.

Breaking free from this cycle requires recognizing procrastination for what it often is: a mask for indecision.

Decide and Accept You Could Be Wrong

In a world painted with shades of gray, the challenge isn't just in the myriad of choices we face, but in the looming specter of potential mistakes.

Sarah, a seasoned manager, often found herself in the labyrinth of decision-making, and with each step, the shadow of being wrong haunted her. She wasn't alone; many grapple with this fear, the trepidation of taking a path only to discover it was not the right one. But then, what truly is the "right" path?

Sarah remembered her early days when decisions were more about reactions, where errors were met with understanding nods, a pat on the back, and the comforting words, "It's okay, you're still learning."

But as she climbed the echelons of her career, she felt that safety net thinning. Every choice now echoed with consequences, with a ripple effect that could influence projects, teams, even the company's future.

But it was during a particularly challenging project that Sarah had an epiphany. Staring at multiple strategies, each with its pros and cons, she realized if the choice were evident, someone else would've taken the helm.

It was precisely because the decision was tough that it was hers to make. And with that realization came another: the possibility of being wrong wasn't just a risk, it was a certainty. Not always, but sometimes. And that was okay.

This acceptance wasn't a resignation to fate but a profound understanding. Sarah recognized that every decision she took was a culmination of her experiences, the data at hand, and her instincts.

If, in the future, it turned out to be a misstep, it wouldn't negate her process; it would simply be a signpost for a different approach next time.

Sarah's shift in perspective transformed not just her approach to decisions but also the culture of her team. They began to view challenges not as pitfalls, but as opportunities.

Errors were no longer just setbacks but learnings. Decisions became faster, innovation thrived, and a newfound resilience permeated the team.

They realized that in the ever-evolving dance of progress, sometimes you lead, sometimes you follow, and sometimes you stumble. But you always keep moving.

In Sarah's journey, there lies a lesson for all. Life isn't about the pursuit of unerring perfection; it's about making choices, embracing the outcomes, and using every experience, good or bad, as a stepping stone towards a better tomorrow. In the embrace of potential errors lies the true courage of decision-making.

If You're in Charge, Make it Clear Who Decides: A Tale of Leadership Clarity

Amidst the buzz of a Monday morning meeting, Martin, the team leader, noticed a pattern. Lately, every decision, big or small, was being tossed around like a hot potato.

Everyone had an opinion, and the discussions, though fruitful, often meandered, losing sight of a conclusion. There was a democratic beauty to it, but also an inefficiency that couldn't be ignored.

One such meeting was pivotal. The team was tasked with choosing a strategy for an upcoming product launch. The stakes were high, and as the discussion began, the room was divided.

Some members were in favor of a soft, phased rollout, while others advocated for a grand launch. The debate raged on, with valid points on both sides.

Martin observed silently, recognizing the depth of insight and passion each team member brought. But as hours passed, the clock was ticking, and no consensus was in sight. The energy in the room began to wane, replaced by a palpable tension.

Realizing the impasse, Martin decided to intervene. "I appreciate the depth and commitment each of you has shown today," he began. "It's clear that we all want the best for this product and our company. But we need to move forward."

He paused, letting his words sink in. "I understand the value of collective decision-making. But sometimes, for the sake of progress and clarity, it's important to remember the structure of our team.

As the leader, the final decision rests with me. I've heard you all, and I will take every viewpoint into consideration. But at the end of the day, I will make the call, and once that call is made, I need everyone onboard."

There was a brief silence, not of resentment, but of understanding. Team members nodded, appreciating Martin's forthrightness. By asserting his role, he hadn't diminished theirs.

Instead, he had clarified the dynamics, ensuring that while everyone had a voice, the responsibility of decision-making rested on defined shoulders.

Post that meeting, the dynamics in Martin's team shifted subtly. Team members felt more empowered to share their insights, knowing that their voices were valued.

But they also recognized the importance of leadership and the responsibility that came with it. Martin, too, was more proactive, ensuring he provided clear directions when needed, while still fostering an environment of collaboration.

Martin's experience underscores a vital leadership lesson. In the dance of teamwork, while collective decision-making has its merits, there are moments where clarity of authority is essential.

Leaders need to strike that delicate balance, ensuring that while everyone feels heard, there's no ambiguity about who makes the final call. Such clarity not only streamlines decisions but also fosters trust and respect within a team.

Indicate That You Are Soliciting Opinion: The Art of Sounding Board Conversations

In the cozy, sunlit corner of a local cafe, Alicia sat with a notepad, scribbling occasionally as she chatted with Marcus, a trusted colleague. Their conversations had often been the bedrock of many decisions Alicia had made over the years. Marcus wasn't just a colleague but a sounding board, providing an outside perspective that Alicia found invaluable.

However, today was slightly different. As Alicia outlined her latest project and its challenges, she prefaced with a clear statement: "Marcus, I'm not looking for a decision from this conversation. I'm sharing this with you because I value your perspective and I need it to balance my own thoughts. I need a sounding board."

By setting this expectation, Alicia had done something essential. She had established the framework for the conversation, indicating its purpose and ensuring that Marcus understood his role. This wasn't about seeking approval or validation but about leveraging another perspective to refine her own thinking.

Marcus nodded, appreciating the clarity. He listened, asked probing questions, challenged some of Alicia's assumptions, and offered insights. But he did so with the understanding that his role was not to decide or persuade but to reflect, clarify, and provide a different lens to view the problem.

This dynamic created a space for genuine dialogue. With the pressures of decision-making removed, the conversation was more about exploration than conclusion. It allowed for divergences and convergences, for uncertainties and clarifications.

Alicia left the cafe that day with a clearer mind, not because she had found an answer, but because she had explored the breadth and depth of her challenge. The sounding board conversation had served its purpose, offering her a richer palette of thoughts to paint her decision.

For leaders and decision-makers, Alicia's approach is a lesson in the nuanced art of conversation. Soliciting opinions is not always about seeking solutions. Sometimes, it's about refining one's own understanding, and for such instances, it's crucial to ensure that those providing input understand their role.

When leaders clarify their need for a sounding board, they establish an environment conducive to open dialogue. This approach ensures they gain diverse perspectives while freeing participants from the burden of meeting expectations. It's a testament to the idea that sometimes, the journey of a conversation is just as valuable as its destination.

26. Viewing The Current Through The Lens Of The Past

Humans naturally gravitate towards the familiar. When faced with challenges, there's an instinctual pull to use solutions that have worked in the past.

If a method was effective previously, it seems reasonable to assume it might be again, offering a sense of security and reducing the perceived risk of venturing into the unknown.

However, this reliance on familiarity can be both a strength and a trap. The world is in a state of constant change, and today's problems might differ from those of yesterday in subtle or significant ways.

By always resorting to what has worked before, there's a risk of overlooking better or more suitable solutions that address the unique intricacies of the current situation. This could potentially hinder progress and stifle adaptability.

Effective problem-solving requires a blend of past experience and openness to new approaches. It's essential to assess if the current problem truly mirrors those from the past. Even if they seem similar on the surface, different contexts or variables might be at play.

Additionally, as time moves on, there might be new techniques, tools, or information available that weren't previously. Balancing the benefits of tried-and-true methods with the potential of innovative approaches ensures that decisions are both informed and adaptable.

In the end, while past experiences are invaluable in guiding our decisions, it's equally crucial to remain receptive to new ideas, ensuring we aren't solely anchored to old methods when navigating contemporary challenges.

The Case of the Failing Bookstore

Julia inherited a quaint, brick-and-mortar bookstore from her grandfather. The store had been running successfully for decades.

When sales began to decline, Julia's initial instinct was to stick to the strategies her grandfather employed, thinking, "It's worked for years. It should still work now."

Her grandfather's approach involved personalized customer service, a well-curated selection of books, and occasional in-store events. For years, these were the secrets to the store's success.

However, the world had changed. Digital platforms were becoming dominant, online retailers offered heavy discounts, and the younger generation's reading habits had shifted.

Instead of merely relying on her grandfather's methods, Julia decided to reassess the situation. While she continued to uphold the store's legacy of excellent customer service and curated book selections, she also recognized the need for modernization.

She introduced an online catalog for the store, started a monthly book subscription box with personalized book choices, and engaged with customers through social media, offering reading suggestions and hosting virtual author meets.

By blending her grandfather's tried-and-true strategies with new digital approaches, Julia revitalized the bookstore. She honored its history while ensuring its relevance in a digital age.

Sometimes Old Solutions Can Be Applied to New Problems

In the ever-evolving landscape of problem-solving, there's a natural inclination towards innovative and novel strategies. As we confront new challenges, fresh perspectives often seem like the most fitting responses. However, looking back at history reveals that many past solutions carry a timeless wisdom, making them apt even for modern predicaments.

Old solutions have often been refined over years, if not centuries, of trial and error. Their longevity is a testament to their effectiveness.

While the context or specifics of a situation might evolve, the fundamental nature of many problems retains a consistent thread. This consistency means that certain traditional solutions can remain pertinent, even when applied to new challenges.

Rather than relegating an old solution to the annals of history, it can be beneficial to adapt and recalibrate it for the present.

By grasping the foundational principles that made a solution effective and modifying it to the nuances of a current problem, it's possible to draw from the reservoir of past knowledge while staying rooted in the present.

Take, for instance, the practice of crop rotation in agriculture. Historically, farmers noted that repeated cultivation of the same crop in a field led to nutrient depletion. To mitigate this, they would change the crop type with each planting season.

In today's world, with increasing concerns about sustainability and the environmental toll of chemical fertilizers, this ancient method has regained prominence.

Contemporary farmers are integrating crop rotation with modern agricultural technology, creating a blend that conserves soil health, minimizes chemical inputs, and promotes sustainable farming.

This fusion of old and new underscores that foundational strategies, when combined with current tools and knowledge, can offer potent solutions.

Drawing from the past doesn't negate the value of innovation; instead, it showcases that a well-rounded approach to problem-solving can involve harmonizing the wisdom of yesteryears with the insights of today.

27. Dealing With Internal Politics

Politics arise naturally within organizations due to differences in interests, values, and power dynamics. As individuals or groups navigate these settings, they inevitably encounter differing goals, priorities, and perspectives, leading to potential conflicts of interest.

This political behavior is also accentuated when there's ambiguity in roles, responsibilities, or rewards, causing people to resort to various tactics to ensure their interests are safeguarded or promoted.

Some individuals gravitate towards confrontation, believing that through it, the best ideas will emerge or that it's the most direct way to get their desired outcomes.

They're forthright about their intentions, and their tactics are overt. Although this approach can occasionally hasten decision-making or result in more refined solutions, unchecked confrontation can contribute to a hostile work environment if not balanced with cooperation and mutual respect.

In contrast, there are those who opt for subtler, more covert tactics. These individuals might engage in spreading rumors, withholding crucial information, or forming undisclosed alliances to push their agendas.

Such underhanded tactics can be particularly detrimental, as they erode trust within teams and organizations. Colleagues might find themselves constantly second-guessing or doubting the motives of others, leading to an atmosphere of suspicion.

The idea that politics intensifies higher up the organizational hierarchy is anchored in the realization that, at elevated levels, there's more at stake. The rewards and risks both amplify, leading to heightened political behavior.

Decisions made at these levels usually have wider implications and impact a more extensive set of stakeholders, introducing more complexities and potential for conflicting interests.

To effectively navigate this intricate political landscape, it's essential to recognize and comprehend its intricacies. Being cognizant of the key players, their motivations, and their modus operandi is crucial.

Establishing genuine relationships and alliances can offer some respite from political maneuverings, as trust and open dialogue can diminish the propensity for politics.

Above all, keeping the broader goals and mission of the organization at the forefront can help steer clear of unnecessary political distractions and maintain focus on what truly matters.

Dealing With "Golden Child" / "Favorite" Issues

Dealing with "golden child" or "favorite" dynamics in organizational settings can be a delicate challenge. These preferences stem from favoritism where certain individuals receive preferential treatment due to personal relationships, shared histories, or tenure within the organization.

Such favoritism can manifest in varied ways, from more significant opportunities to casual high regard in conversations. While it's natural for individuals to have biases, unchecked favoritism in a professional environment can undermine team morale and fairness.

For individuals outside of the favored circle, the journey can feel like an uphill battle. Even if you bring competence and dedication to the table, the shadow of favoritism can seem to set you a few steps back.

One way to navigate this is by focusing intently on the quality and consistency of your work. When your contributions consistently shine, it's harder for them to be overshadowed by biases.

Open communication can also be a valuable tool. If you're feeling sidelined due to perceived favoritism, consider addressing it with your supervisor. However, approach the conversation with care, focusing on your aspirations and the opportunities you seek rather than leveling accusations.

Feedback is another powerful ally. By actively seeking it, you not only refine your skills but also demonstrate a commitment to growth and excellence. Pair this with efforts to diversify your professional relationships within the organization. Having allies and acquaintances in various departments can provide a broader perspective and improve visibility.

Investing in your professional development, such as by attending workshops or seeking mentorships, can also help counterbalance the effects of favoritism. It sends a clear message about your commitment to your role and growth.

Lastly, resilience is key. Navigating professional landscapes, especially those colored by favoritism, requires an understanding that personal worth isn't tied to one's relative position to the "golden child."

Staying focused, seeking feedback, and nurturing a diverse professional network, one can not only navigate but also thrive amid such challenges.

Combatting *"We've always done it that way"*

Combatting the "We've always done it that way" mindset is a frequent challenge, especially in established organizations.

This sentiment often becomes a barrier to innovation and can stymie attempts to implement more efficient or effective procedures. Such resistance is rooted in various factors, from the comfort of routine to the fear of the unknown.

Historically, humans are creatures of habit. Established routines offer predictability, which in turn provides a sense of security. For many, especially in larger organizations, established methods represent tested pathways that have consistently delivered results.

Therefore, any suggestion to alter or replace them can be met with apprehension.

This apprehension might be due to concerns about the risks of new methods, or even just the energy and effort required to learn something new.

For individuals or teams keen on driving change, understanding the root of this resistance is the first step. Recognizing that such hesitations aren't always about obstinacy, but often about genuine concerns or deeply ingrained habits, can guide more empathetic and effective strategies for change.

One approach is to demonstrate the benefits of the proposed change. By providing clear evidence that a new method is superior, whether in terms of efficiency, cost-effectiveness, or outcomes, you can make a compelling case. Piloting the change on a smaller scale can provide tangible results to showcase to skeptics.

Engaging stakeholders early in the process can also be beneficial. When individuals feel involved in the decision-making process and understand the reasons behind a change, they're more likely to support it.

Encouraging open dialogues where concerns can be voiced and addressed can foster a more collaborative environment.

Additionally, offering training and resources can ease the transition. One of the major hurdles to change is the learning curve associated with new processes. By providing the necessary tools and training, you can alleviate some of the apprehensions associated with the unknown.

Lastly, it's important to acknowledge and celebrate small wins. As new methods or processes are adopted, highlighting their successes can build momentum for broader organizational changes.

Are You a Caesar or a Brutus?

Amidst the buzzing hive of Acme Corp, two figures stood out: Marcus, the company's golden boy, heralded for his achievements and innovation, and Karl, a colleague from the same division but always lurking just a bit in the shadow.

While Marcus, with his charismatic personality and proven track record, was seen by many as the company's 'Caesar', there were whispered concerns about Karl, whose ambition was said to sometimes override his loyalty.

At company gatherings, Karl often toasted to Marcus, praising his vision for the company's future. Yet, in the dimly lit corners of office hallways and over hushed coffee breaks, it was rumored that Karl was weaving a different narrative—one that painted Marcus as out of touch, complacent, or even deceitful.

A few close to Karl noted his subtle tactics: a raised eyebrow here, a vague insinuation there, a carefully worded question planted in the right ear. Karl was skilled in the art of suggestion, able to plant seeds of doubt without overtly appearing to do so.

Marcus, for his part, remained oblivious. In his eyes, every member of the team, including Karl, was pulling in the same direction, aiming for the collective success of Acme Corp.

It was this trust, perhaps naive, that left him vulnerable. He never imagined that someone from his own ranks, a 'Brutus', might be subtly undermining him.

As months went by, these whisper campaigns began to take a toll. Projects Marcus spearheaded were met with unexpected resistance. Trusted allies started to distance themselves, influenced by the whispers they heard. All the while, Karl watched from the sidelines, waiting for his moment to step into the spotlight.

Ella, a longtime employee of Acme Corp and a keen observer, saw the shifting sands beneath Marcus's feet. She had seen this play out before: the rising star, the envious colleague, the downfall orchestrated through rumors. Determined not to let history repeat itself, she approached Marcus with her concerns.

At first, Marcus struggled to believe Ella's words. The idea that Karl, a colleague he had shared countless projects and successes with, could be working against him was a bitter pill to swallow. But as he reflected on recent events, the pieces began to fall into place.

The story of Caesar and Brutus is an old one, echoing through the ages. In the modern halls of corporations like Acme Corp, the same dynamics play out, albeit in subtler forms.

The narrative serves as a cautionary tale about the vulnerabilities that come with success and the hidden agendas that can lurk behind friendly facades.

In the end, forewarned is forearmed. Marcus, now alerted to the undercurrents surrounding him, took steps to address the issue directly, seeking open communication and transparency.

The resolution of this modern-day drama remains to be seen, but one thing is certain: the shadows of ancient Rome still cast their influence on the complex interplay of ambition, loyalty, and power in today's corporate world.

It's Not Always Politics

In the intricate web of organizational decision-making, it's easy to jump to the conclusion that every decision is influenced by politics. After all, in many settings, politics can play a significant role.

However, it's crucial to recognize that not every decision stems from political motivations. At times, decisions are made based purely on the merit of the situation or the specific needs of the organization at that moment.

Imagine a scenario where a company decides to pivot its marketing strategy, opting for a new approach that sidelines some ongoing projects.

The teams behind those projects might feel marginalized or speculate that the shift was a result of internal politics or favoritism. However, it's entirely possible that the decision was made based on data, market trends, or a genuine belief that the new direction would be more effective for the company's goals.

Decisions, especially in large organizations, are multifaceted. They're often the result of extensive deliberations, weighing pros and cons, considering short-term impacts against long-term benefits, and analyzing a plethora of data and input from various stakeholders.

Just because the outcome might not align with everyone's preferences or expectations doesn't inherently mean it was politically driven.

In fact, viewing every decision through a political lens can be counterproductive. It can sow seeds of distrust, hamper open communication, and create an atmosphere of skepticism.

It's essential for team members to give the benefit of the doubt and seek clarity rather than immediately attributing decisions to politics. Open dialogue can often reveal the rationale behind decisions, helping dispel myths and misconceptions.

In the world of corporate decision-making, while politics can undoubtedly play a part, it's not the sole driver.

More often than not, decisions are made with the organization's best interest at heart, aiming to navigate the complex landscape of market dynamics, resources, and opportunities. Recognizing and appreciating this distinction fosters a healthier, more transparent, and collaborative work environment.

It's Not Always Personal

In the rapidly evolving landscape of businesses and organizations, change is inevitable. As companies adapt to new technologies, market dynamics, and efficiency models, decisions are often made to align with the broader strategic vision.

However, these decisions, while strategic at their core, can deeply impact individuals or entire departments. It's essential to understand that, in many cases, these decisions are not rooted in personal biases or evaluations but rather in the overarching needs of the organization.

Take the example of a company choosing to replace its in-house Quality Assurance department with an outsourced group. On the surface, this could seem like a direct critique of the in-house team's competence or value.

In reality, the decision might stem from various factors, such as the need to cut costs in a competitive market, the ability to tap into specialized expertise, or the flexibility that comes with outsourced teams in scaling operations up or down based on project requirements.

For the members of the in-house QA team, such a decision can be heart-wrenching. Their dedication, years of service, and commitment to the company come into stark contrast with the cold, calculated nature of business decisions. It's natural to feel hurt, marginalized, or even betrayed.

However, it's vital to separate the individual or the team's value from the decision itself. These organizational choices are often driven by broader financial or strategic imperatives that go beyond the performance or capabilities of a particular team. It doesn't negate the team's contributions in the past or diminish their professional worth.

For leaders and decision-makers, communication is key in such scenarios.

Being transparent about the reasons behind significant changes, and ensuring that affected teams or individuals are supported through transitions, can mitigate feelings of resentment or confusion.

It's crucial to acknowledge the contributions of those affected, provide avenues for feedback, and, if possible, offer alternative roles or support in transitioning to new opportunities.

"…And Sometimes It Is"

In the intricate dance of organizational dynamics, there are moments when decisions aren't merely strategic but deeply personal.

At times, an individual can become the center of a political maelstrom, where decisions seem to pivot around or directly target them. This could arise from clashing ideologies, perceived threats to existing power structures, or merely being on the unintended side of a political divide.

Accepting such an outcome, especially when it feels like a direct affront, is challenging. It's essential first to pause and reflect upon the situation.

Could there have been any actions or choices that might have contributed to this outcome? Sometimes, we might inadvertently play a role in situations, even if we don't realize it.

Speaking with trusted colleagues or mentors can provide clarity. Their perspectives might shed light on the political nature of the decision or give insights into other underlying factors.

While it's natural to feel slighted, it's crucial to concentrate on areas of life and work where influence and control are tangible. Drowning in the perceived injustice of a situation won't alter the outcome; it's more productive to channel energies into areas that can foster growth and change.

Change, even when imposed, can sometimes lead to unexpected opportunities. It might usher in new experiences, challenges, and avenues for personal and professional development.

It's essential to avoid getting ensnared in a web of negativity. While expressing hurt or frustration is natural, indulging in prolonged negative discussions or actions can be draining and counterproductive.

Sharing feelings with friends, family, or professionals can be therapeutic. It offers a way to process emotions and navigate the turbulent waters of change. Plotting the next steps, whether seeking a new role, exploring a different field, or diving into a fresh project, can provide direction and a sense of purpose.

Ultimately, the goal is acceptance. Not necessarily agreeing with what transpired but acknowledging it as a step towards moving forward. Past grievances can act as chains, holding one back from potential growth and opportunities.

It's imperative to remember that a single decision, no matter how political or personal, doesn't encapsulate one's entire worth or capabilities.

Often, resilience shines brightest when forged in the fires of adversity. The journey forward is not just about overcoming but thriving despite the odds.